Diabetic Cookies

· ·

Mary Jane Finsand

Foreword by
James D. Healy, M.D., F.A.A.P.

STERLING PUBLISHING CO., INC.
NEW YORK

Edited by Laurel Ornitz
Recipe consultant: Carol Tiffany

Library of Congress Cataloging-in-Publication Data
Finsand, Mary Jane.
    Diabetic cookies / Mary Jane Finsand ; foreword by James D.
Healy.
        p.   cm.
    Includes index.
    ISBN 0-8069-0506-9
    1. Diabetes—Diet therapy—Recipes.   2. Cookies.   I. Title.
RC662.F5653   1994
641.8'654—dc20   93-43893
                                                                  CIP

10   9   8   7   6   5   4   3

Published by Sterling Publishing Company, Inc.
387 Park Avenue South, New York, N.Y. 10016
© 1994 by Mary Jane Finsand
Distributed in Canada by Sterling Publishing
% Canadian Manda Group, P.O. Box 920, Station U
Toronto, Ontario, Canada M8Z 5P9
Distributed in Great Britain and Europe by Cassell PLC
Villiers House, 41/47 Strand, London WC2N 5JE, England
Distributed in Australia by Capricorn Link (Australia) Pty Ltd.
P.O. Box 6651, Baulkham Hills, Business Centre, NSW 2153, Australia
Manufactured in the United States of America
All rights reserved

Sterling ISBN 0-8069-0506-9

Contents

Publisher's Note

Mary Jane Finsand passed away in late 1993. I regard her untimely death as a great loss of both an author and a friend. For almost 15 years, we published diabetic cookbooks together, 11 in all, many best-sellers, and all written with the accuracy and time-tested recipes that were her trademark. Her unflagging optimism and sunny disposition never wavered, even in her last battle against cancer. This final book, finished but a few weeks before her death, exemplifies her commitment and dedication to her work. All her many readers and her friends at Sterling will miss her.

Charles Nurnberg
Senior Vice President
Sterling Publishing Co., Inc.

Foreword

Users of Mary Jane Finsand's other diabetic cookbooks know that diabetics can eat a wide variety of delicious foods and still follow a doctor-prescribed diet. With the *Diabetic Cookie Cookbook*, Mary Jane has created recipes for scrumptious cookies that really tempt the palate.

Each recipe in this cookbook includes calories, carbohydrates, and food exchanges for each cookie. This completeness allows diabetics and other individuals to regulate food intake within medically prescribed recommendations.

Although written specifically for the diabetic, this cookbook is an excellent resource for people who like to eat desserts and still follow recommended nutritional guidelines.

James D. Healy, M.D., F.A.A.P.

A Note from Covenant Medical Center

With the *Diabetic Cookie Cookbook*, people with diabetes can enjoy cookies in their diet and still control their blood-glucose levels. However, these recipes are not just for diabetics on the exchange diet, as calculations are included for diabetics and others on the carbohydrate system.

Your friends and relatives who aren't diabetic will enjoy these cookies too. For the diabetic, occasionally include these cookies in your menu planning, especially for social or family functions.

We want to remind you that these cookies need to be substituted into the diabetic meal plan. If you don't have a diabetic meal plan appropriate to your life-style, we encourage you to contact a registered dietician.

Mary Steffensmeier, R.D.
Lynette Gersema, R.D.
Covenant Medical Center
Waterloo, Iowa

Introduction

Cookies—whether dropped, formed, pressed, or rolled—are always a favorite. They're quick and easy to make, and their endless variety of ingredients makes them interesting to bake. Many of my readers have asked for a complete cookie cookbook. Here it is. From peanut butter or chocolate chip to pfeffernuss or spritz, this collection offers a delightful array of treats to serve the diabetic or any one of your family or friends.

When I chose recipes for this book, I aimed for variety. Also, I wanted you to be able to bake several different recipes at the same time; therefore, I tried to make many of the exchanges and calories equal for a number of different recipes. You can bake a variety of cookies with the same exchanges, use a few cookies from each recipe, and then freeze the rest for another day.

Not surprisingly, many of the recipes are old favorites, which I converted to meet the needs of the diabetic. There are simple recipes for cookies that children will enjoy making as much as eating. There are cookies especially well suited for bake sales or large social gatherings. There are dozens of recipes developed for an everyday treat as well as an assortment for holidays.

Don't wait—create a batch of homemade cookies today. They're always a welcome treat.

Mary Jane Finsand

Sugar & Sugar Replacements

Most sweeteners or sugar replacements are available in your supermarket. They vary in sweetness, aftertaste, aroma, and calories. The listing below is by ingredient name rather than by product name. Check the side of the box or bottle to determine the contents of the product.

Aspartame and aspartame products are fairly new additions to supermarket shelves. Aspartame is a natural protein sweetener. Because of its intense sweetness, it reduces calories and carbohydrates in the diet. Aspartame has a sweet aroma and no aftertaste. It seems to complement some of the other sweeteners by removing their bitter aftertaste. Aspartame does lose some of its sweetness in heating and is therefore recommended for use in cold products.

Cyclamates and products containing cyclamates are not as sweet as saccharin and saccharin products, and cyclamates also leave a bitter aftertaste. Many sugar replacements are a combination of saccharin and cyclamates.

Fructose is commonly known as fruit sugar. It is actually a natural sugar found in fruits and honey. Fructose tastes the same as common table sugar (sucrose), but because of its intense sweetness it reduces calories and carbohydrates in the diet. It isn't affected by heating or cooling, but fructose tends to add moisture to baked products.

Glycyrrhizen and products containing glycyrrhizen are as sweet as saccharin and saccharin products. They are seen less in supermarkets because they tend to give food a licorice taste and aroma.

Saccharin and products containing saccharin are the most widely known and used of the intense sweeteners. When used in baking or cooking, saccharin has a lingering bitter aftertaste. You will normally find it in the form of sodium saccharin in products labelled low-calorie sugar replacements. Granular, or dry, sugar replacements containing sodium saccharin give less of an aftertaste to foods that are heated. But it's best to use liquid sugar replacements containing sodium saccharin in cold foods or in foods that have partially cooled and no longer need any heating.

Sorbitol is used in many commercial food products. It has little or no aftertaste and a sweet aroma. At present it can only be bought in bulk form at health-food outlets.

If you have difficulty finding these products, try to contact a distributor or a mail-order outlet.

The individual consumer should write to:

The Fruitful Yield
2111 N. Bloomingdale Road
Glendale Heights, IL 60139

or

T & K Health Foods
1429 West Third St.
Waterloo, IA 50701

For health-food retailers or other large orders, write or call:

NOW Natural Foods
2000 Bloomingdale Road
Glendale Heights, IL 60139
(708) 893–1330

Using the Recipes—Conversion Guides, Flavorings & Extracts, Spices & Herbs

All of the recipes have been developed using granulated fructose and/or a granulated sugar replacement; diet products for syrups, toppings, puddings, and gelatins; and imitation or low-calorie dairy and nondairy products.

All use a sweetener or sugar replacement that has the same amount of sweetness as regular sugar. If you use a stronger product, use it in proportion to the equivalencies of that product. Remember, don't bake with an aspartame sweetener.

Read the recipes carefully; then assemble all the equipment and ingredients. Use standard measuring equipment (whether metric or customary), and be sure to measure accurately.

Customary Terms

t.	teaspoon	qt.	quart
T.	tablespoon	oz.	ounce
c.	cup	lb.	pound
pkg.	package	°F	degrees Fahrenheit
pt.	pint	in.	inch

Metric Symbols

mL	millilitre	°C	degrees Celsius
L	litre	mm	millimetre
g	gram	cm	centimetre
kg	kilogram		

Guide to Approximate Equivalents

Customary				Metric	
Ounces Pounds	Cups	Tablespoons	Teaspoons	Millilitres	Grams Kilograms
			¼ t.	1 mL	1 g
			½ t.	2 mL	
			1 t.	5 mL	
			2 t.	10 mL	
½ oz.		1 T.	3 t.	15 mL	14 g
1 oz.		2 T.	6 t.	30 mL	28 g
2 oz.	¼ c.	4 T.	12 t.	60 mL	
4 oz.	½ c.	8 T.	24 t.	125 mL	
8 oz.	1 c.	16 T.	48 t.	250 mL	
2.2 lb.					1 kg

Keep in mind that this guide doesn't show exact conversions, but it can be used in a general way for food measurement.

Conversion Guide for Cooking Pans and Casseroles

Customary	Metric
1 qt.	1 L
2 qt.	2 L
3 qt.	3 L

Candy-Thermometer Guide

Use this guide to test for doneness.

Fahrenheit °F	Test		Celsius °C
230–234°	Syrup:	Thread	100–112°
234–240°	Fondant/Fudge:	Soft ball	112–115°
244–248°	Caramels:	Firm ball	118–120°
250–266°	Marshmallows:	Hard Ball	121–130°
270–290°	Taffy:	Soft crack	132–143°
300–310°	Brittle:	Hard crack	149–154°

Oven-Cooking Guides

Fahrenheit °F	Oven Heat	Celsius °C
250–275°	very slow	120–135°
300–325°	slow	150–165°
350–375°	moderate	175–190°
400–425°	hot	200–220°
450–475°	very hot	230–245°
475–500°	hottest	250–290°

Guide to Baking-Pan Sizes

Customary	Metric	Holds	Holds (Metric)
8-in. pie	20-cm pie	2 c.	600 mL
9-in. pie	23-cm pie	1 qt.	1 L
10-in. pie	25-cm pie	1¼ qt.	1.3 L
8-in. round	20-cm round	1 qt.	1 L
9-in. round	23-cm round	1½ qt.	1.5 L
8-in. square	20-cm square	2 qt.	2 L
9-in. square	23-cm square	2½ qt.	2.5 L
9 × 5 × 2 in. loaf	23 × 13 × 5 cm loaf	2 qt.	2 L
9-in. tube	23-cm tube	3 qt.	3 L
10-in. tube	25-cm tube	3 qt.	3 L
10-in. Bundt	25-cm Bundt	3 qt.	3 L
9 × 5 in.	23 × 13 cm	1½ qt.	1.5 L
10 × 6 in.	25 × 16 cm	3½ qt.	3.5 L
11 × 7 in.	27 × 17 cm	3½ qt.	3.5 L
13 × 9 × 2 in.	33 × 23 × 5 cm	3½ qt.	3.5 L
14 × 10 in.	36 × 25 cm	cookie tin	
15½ × 10½ × 1 in.	39 × 25 × 3 cm	jelly roll	

Flavorings & Extracts

Choose from the following to give your recipes some zip, without adding calories.

Almond	Butter rum	Pecan
Anise (Licorice)	Cherry	Peppermint
Apricot	Chocolate	Pineapple
Banana creme	Coconut	Raspberry
Blackberry	Grape	Rum
Black walnut	Hazelnut	Sassafras
Blueberry	Lemon	Sherry
Brandy	Lime	Strawberry
Butter	Mint	Vanilla
Butternut	Orange	Walnut

Spices & Herbs

Allspice: cinnamon-ginger-nutmeg flavor

Anise: licorice flavor

Cinnamon: pungent, sweet flavor

Cloves: pungent, sweet flavor

Coriander: butter-lemon flavor

Ginger: strong, pungent flavor

Nutmeg: sweet, nutty flavor

Cookie-Baking Utensils

There are only a few basic utensils you'll need for baking perfect cookies. You won't need all of the utensils for every recipe.

Baking pans: Standard baking pans are used in all the recipes. Always use shiny, metal baking pans. They reflect oven heat away from the cookies and produce even browning.

Cookie cutters: Cookie cutters come in many shapes. They're used for rolled cookies. They should be sharp and dipped in flour before use.

Cookie sheets: You'll need at least two cookie sheets. When shopping for cookie sheets, try to find shiny, heavy-gauge, aluminum sheets with low or no sides. If you have trouble finding heavy-gauge sheets, buy a lighter weight, but make sure the cookie sheets are shiny. The sheets should be flat, or have one or two sides raised for easy handling. They shouldn't crowd your oven.

Cookie press: A cookie press is a metal, tube-shaped utensil with several attachments for making cookies of various shapes. They are available in electric or hand-crank models.

Cooling racks: You will need at least two good-size cooling racks.

Electric mixer: An electric mixer is recommended for recipes that require thorough beating. However, many of the recipes can be done by hand.

Flour sifter: A sifter is needed to help mix dry ingredients together. You must use a sifter even when the flour states that it's pre-sifted.

Measuring cups and spoons: You'll need at least one set of standard measuring cups and spoons. For dry ingredients, metal or plastic cups are used. For measuring liquids, use glass or plastic cups with the measurements marked on the sides.

Mixing bowls: You'll need a range of mixing bowls from small to large.

Pastry blender: A pastry blender is a wire utensil used for cutting solid shortenings into dry ingredients. If you don't have one, use two table knives.

Pastry cloth and stockinet: A pastry cloth helps you roll out cookie dough easily, because the dough is less likely to stick to the cloth than it would be to a hard surface. A pastry stockinet fits over a rolling pin.

Rolling pin: Select a rolling pin that fits comfortably in your hands.

Rubber or plastic spatula: Always select a flexible spatula. The spatula is used when beating for scraping cookie dough down from the sides of the bowl.

Types of Cookie

Drop cookies are among the easiest types of cookie to bake. They come in a large variety of flavors. The soft dough for drop cookies is usually dropped or pushed into small mounds directly onto the cookie sheet. The cookie sheet should be cool when you drop the cookies. Be sure to allow space between cookie-dough mounds, because drop cookies tend to spread.

Bar cookies are a combination of a cookie and a cake. The dough is spread or pressed into baking pans. After baking, the cookies should be allowed to cool in the pan and then cut into bars.

Moulded, or hand-shaped, cookies are made by using your hands to shape stiff dough into balls, patties, or ropes. A ball of dough can either be baked as it is or flattened with the tongs of a fork or the bottom of a glass. It's easier to mould these cookies if you flour your hands beforehand.

Pressed, or spritz, cookies are shaped by forcing dough through a cookie press into various shapes.

Icebox, or refrigerator, cookies are wrapped in plastic wrap, waxed paper, or aluminum foil, then thoroughly chilled before cutting and baking. The advantage of these cookies is that you can cut only the number of cookies you need and return the remaining dough to the refrigerator.

Rolled cookies are similar to refrigerator cookies in that the dough is normally chilled before it's rolled on a floured surface and cut into shapes. When making rolled cookies, roll out only a small amount of dough, and return the remaining dough to the refrigerator.

Drop Cookies

Chocolate Fruit Drops

1 T.	margarine, melted	15 L
1 oz.	unsweetened baking chocolate, melted	28 g
¼ c.	granulated fructose	60 mL
1	egg, slightly beaten	1
½ c. + 2 T.	all-purpose flour	155 mL
½ t.	cream of tartar	2 mL
¼ t.	baking soda	1 mL
⅓ c.	unsweetened dried mixed fruit*	90 mL

*Unsweetened dried mixed fruit can be bought at health-food stores.

Combine melted margarine and chocolate in a bowl. Add fructose and egg. Stir until completely mixed. Add flour, cream of tartar, and baking soda. Stir until blended. Stir in dried fruit. Drop small balls of the cookie dough onto an ungreased cookie sheet. Bake at 350°F (175°C) for 10 minutes. Remove from cookie sheet immediately.

Yield: 24 cookies
Exchange, 1 cookie: ⅓ bread
Calories, 1 cookie: 27
Carbohydrates, 1 cookie: 4 g

Apple & Raisin Cookies

⅓ c.	unsweetened applesauce	90 mL
1	egg	1
1 t.	vanilla extract	5 mL
1 c.	all-purpose flour	250 mL

2 T.	granulated sugar replacement	30 mL
1 t.	baking powder	5 mL
½ c.	diced apple	125 mL
¼ c.	chopped raisins	60 mL

Combine applesauce, egg, and vanilla in a medium-size bowl. Beat with a fork until thoroughly blended. Thoroughly stir in flour, sugar replacement, and baking powder. Stir in apple pieces and chopped raisins. Spray cookie sheet lightly with a vegetable-oil spray. Drop cookie dough onto the greased cookie sheet. Bake at 350°F (175°C) for 10 to 12 minutes. Cookies will be white; don't try to brown them. Remove from cookie sheet, and cool.

Yield: 24 cookies
Exchange, 1 cookie: ⅓ bread
Calories, 1 cookie: 30
Carbohydrates, 1 cookie: 5 g

Oatmeal Mounds

1 T.	margarine, melted	15 mL
¼ c.	granulated fructose	60 mL
¼ c.	apple juice	60 mL
1	egg	1
½ t.	vanilla extract	2 mL
1 c.	all-purpose flour	250 mL
½ t.	cream of tartar	2 mL
¼ t.	baking soda	1 mL
1 c.	quick-cooking oatmeal	250 mL

Combine melted margarine and fructose in a medium-size bowl. Stir to blend. Add apple juice, egg, and vanilla extract. With a fork, beat until thoroughly mixed. Beat in flour, cream of tartar, and baking soda. Stir in oatmeal. Drop in mounds on an ungreased cookie sheet. Bake at 350°F (175°C) for 10 to 12 minutes or until very lightly browned. Remove from cookie sheet immediately. Cool on rack.

Yield: 24 cookies
Exchange, 1 cookie: ½ bread
Calories, 1 cookie: 42
Carbohydrates, 1 cookie: 8 g

Oatmeal Mounds with Raisins

1 T.	margarine, melted	15 mL
¼ c.	granulated fructose	60 mL
¼ c.	apple juice	60 mL
1	egg	1
½ t.	vanilla extract	2 mL
1 c.	all-purpose flour	250 mL
½ t.	cream of tartar	2 mL
¼ t.	baking soda	1 mL
1 c.	quick-cooking oatmeal	250 mL
⅓ c.	raisins	90 mL
2 qt.	boiling water	2 L

Combine melted margarine and fructose in a medium-size bowl. Stir to blend. Add apple juice, egg, and vanilla extract. With a fork, beat until thoroughly mixed. Beat in flour, cream of tartar, and baking soda. Stir in oatmeal. Place raisins in a strainer, and pour boiling water over the raisins. Drain, pat raisins dry, and chop them. Stir raisins into cookie mixture. Drop in mounds on an ungreased cookie sheet. Bake at 350°F (175°C) for 10 to 12 minutes or until very lightly browned. Remove from cookie sheet immediately. Cool on rack.

Yield: 30 cookies
Exchange, 1 cookie: ½ bread
Calories, 1 cookie: 45
Carbohydrates, 1 cookie: 9 g

Spicy Hermits

1 T.	margarine, melted	15 L
¼ c.	granulated fructose	60 mL
¼ c.	hot water	60 mL
2 T.	instant-coffee powder	30 mL
1	egg, slightly beaten	1
1⅓ c.	all-purpose flour	340 mL
½ t.	cream of tartar	2 mL
¼ t.	baking soda	1 mL
½ t.	ground cinnamon	2 mL
¼ t.	ground nutmeg	1 mL

| ¼ t. | ground cloves | 1 mL |
| ¼ c. | chopped raisins | 60 mL |

Stir melted margarine. Add fructose, hot water, and coffee powder. Stir until completely mixed. Beat in egg. Add flour, cream of tartar, baking soda, and spices. Stir until blended. Stir in raisins. Drop cookie dough onto an ungreased cookie sheet. Bake at 350°F (175°C) for 10 to 12 minutes. Remove from cookie sheet immediately.

Yield: 30 cookies
Exchange, 1 cookie: ⅓ bread
Calories, 1 cookie: 28
Carbohydrates, 1 cookie: 6 g

Fairy Drops

⅓ c.	unsweeted applesauce	90 mL
2	egg whites	2
1 t.	vanilla extract	5 mL
½ t.	almond flavoring	2 mL
1 c.	all-purpose flour	250 mL
2 T.	granulated sugar replacement	30 mL
1 T.	ground cardamom	15 mL
½ t.	cream of tartar	2 mL
¼ t.	baking soda	1 mL

Combine applesauce, egg whites, vanilla, and almond flavoring in a medium-size bowl. Beat with a fork until thoroughly blended. Combine flour, sugar replacement, cardamom, cream of tartar, and baking soda in a sifter. Sift onto a piece of waxed paper; pour back into sifter and sift again. Pour flour mixture back into sifter, and sift directly into the applesauce mixture. Beat with a fork until well blended. Mixture will be sticky. Cover and chill for at least one hour or until needed. Spray cookie sheet lightly with a vegetable-oil spray. Drop cookie dough onto the greased cookie sheet. Bake at 375°F (190°C) for 12 to 15 minutes. Remove from cookie sheet and cool.

Yield: 24 cookies
Exchange, 1 cookie: ⅓ bread
Calories, 1 cookie: 20
Carbohydrates, 1 cookie: 4 g

Chocolate Oatmeal Cookies

1 T.	margarine, melted	15 L
1 oz.	unsweetened baking chocolate, melted	28 g
¼ c.	granulated fructose	60 mL
1	egg, slightly beaten	1
½ c.	all-purpose flour	125 mL
3 T.	quick-cooking oatmeal	45 mL
½ t.	cream of tartar	2 mL
¼ t.	baking soda	1 mL

Stir melted margarine and chocolate until blended. Add fructose and egg. Stir until completely mixed. Add flour, oatmeal, cream of tartar, and baking soda. Stir until blended. Drop small balls of the cookie dough onto an ungreased cookie sheet. Bake at 350°F (175°C) for 10 minutes. Remove from cookie sheet immediately.

Yield: 24 cookies
Exchange, 1 cookie: ⅓ bread
Calories, 1 cookie: 28
Carbohydrates, 1 cookie: 4 g

Raspberry Chocolate Drops

1 c.	frozen or fresh raspberries	250 mL
1 T.	margarine	15 mL
2 T.	granulated sugar replacement	30 mL
1 T.	granulated fructose	15 mL
1 oz.	unsweetened premelted baking chocolate	28 g
1 T.	fat-free cream cheese	15 mL
½ t.	vanilla extract	2 mL
2	egg whites	2
1½ c.	all-purpose flour	375 mL
1 t.	baking powder	5 mL
½ t.	cream of tartar	2 mL
¼ t.	baking soda	1 mL

Place frozen raspberries in a microwave bowl. Cook in the microwave on HIGH for 1½ minutes or until raspberries are thawed. Mash with a fork. Add margarine and return to microwave for 1 to 2 minutes or until margarine is melted and raspberries are warm. Allow to cool slightly. Beat in sugar replacement, fructose, baking chocolate, cream cheese, vanilla, and egg whites. Stir in flour, baking powder, cream of tartar, and baking soda. Spray cookie sheets lightly with a vegetable-oil spray. Drop cookie dough onto greased cookie sheets. Bake at 375°F (190°C) for 10 to 12 minutes. Remove from cookie sheets, and cool on racks.

Yield: 42 cookies
Exchange, 1 cookie: ¼ bread
Calories, 1 cookie: 21
Carbohydrates, 1 cookie: 3 g

Apricot Oatmeal Cookies

1½ c.	all-purpose flour	375 mL
1 t.	ground cinnamon	5 mL
¾ t.	baking soda	4 mL
½ t.	baking powder	2 mL
½ t.	salt	2 mL
¾ c.	soft margarine	190 mL
⅔ c.	granulated sugar replacement	180 mL
⅓ c.	granulated fructose	90 mL
2	eggs	2
3 T.	sour milk or buttermilk	45 mL
½ c.	dried apricots	125 mL
3 c.	quick-cooking oatmeal	750 mL

Sift together flour, cinnamon, baking soda, baking powder, and salt. Set aside. Using an electric mixer, cream together margarine, sugar replacement, and fructose. Add eggs, one at a time, beating well after each addition. Beat in sifted flour mixture, alternating with sour milk. Using a pair of kitchen scissors, cut apricots into thin strips. Place apricots in a small saucepan with ½ c. (125 mL) water. Bring to a boil over high heat; then reduce heat and simmer, uncovered, until apricots are soft. Add extra water if needed. Drain apricots well and pat dry with paper towels. Stir apricots and oatmeal into cookie dough. Drop dough on lightly greased cookie sheets. Bake at 350°F (175°C) for 10 to 12 minutes or until golden brown. Move to cooling racks.

Yield: 84 cookies
Exchange, 1 cookie: ⅓ bread, ⅓ fat
Calories, 1 cookie: 42
Carbohydrates, 1 cookie: 4 g

Vanilla Pillow Puffs

⅓ c.	unsweetened applesauce	90 mL
1	egg	1
1 t.	vanilla extract	5 mL
1 c.	all-purpose flour	250 mL
2 T.	granulated sugar replacement	30 mL
1 t.	baking powder	5 mL

Combine applesauce, egg, and vanilla in a medium-size bowl. Beat mixture with a fork until thoroughly blended. Thoroughly stir in flour, sugar replacement, and baking powder. Mixture will be sticky. Spray cookie sheet lightly with a vegetable-oil spray. Drop cookie dough onto the greased cookie sheet. Bake at 350°F (175°C) for 10 to 12 minutes. Cookies will be white; don't try to brown them. Remove from cookie sheet and cool.

Yield: 24 cookies
Exchange, 1 cookie: ⅓ bread
Calories, 1 cookie: 23
Carbohydrates, 1 cookie: 4 g

Chocolate Pillow Puffs

⅓ c.	unsweetened applesauce	90 mL
1 oz.	unsweetened baking chocolate, melted	28 g
1	egg	1
1 t.	vanilla extract	5 mL
1 c.	all-purpose flour	250 mL
2 T.	granulated sugar replacement	30 mL
1 t.	baking powder	5 mL

Combine applesauce, melted baking chocolate, egg, and vanilla in a medium-size bowl. Beat with a fork until thoroughly blended. Thoroughly stir in flour, sugar replacement, and baking powder. Mixture will be sticky. Spray cookie sheet lightly with a vegetable-oil spray. Drop cookie dough onto the greased cookie sheet. Bake at 350°F (175°C) for 10 to 12 minutes. Remove from cookie sheet and cool.

Yield: 24 cookies
Exchange, 1 cookie: ⅓ bread, ¼ fat
Calories, 1 cookie: 29
Carbohydrates, 1 cookie: 4 g

Chocolate Pecan Drops

1 T.	margarine, melted	15 L
1 oz.	unsweetened baking chocolate, melted	28 g
¼ c.	granulated fructose	60 mL
1	egg, slightly beaten	1
½ c. + 2 T.	all-purpose flour	155 mL
½ t.	cream of tartar	2 mL
¼ t.	baking soda	1 mL
24	pecan halves	24

Stir melted margarine and chocolate until blended. Add fructose and egg. Stir until completely mixed. Add flour, cream of tartar, and baking soda. Stir until blended. Drop small balls of the cookie dough onto an ungreased cookie sheet. Bake at 350°F (175°C) for 5 minutes. Remove from oven, and press a pecan half into the top of each cookie. Continue baking for 5 minutes more. Remove from cookie sheet immediately.

Yield: 24 cookies
Exchange, 1 cookie: ¼ bread
Calories, 1 cookie: 22
Carbohydrates, 1 cookie: 4 g

Apricot-Snack Cookies

6-oz. jar	baby-food apricot purée	170-g jar
¼ c.	frozen orange-juice concentrate	60 mL
1 T.	granulated fructose	15 mL
1	egg, slightly beaten	1
1 t.	vanilla extract	5 mL
1 c.	all-purpose flour	250 mL
1 t.	baking powder	5 mL

Combine apricot purée, orange-juice concentrate, and fructose in a medium-size bowl. Stir to blend completely. Add egg and vanilla. Beat to mix. Add flour and baking powder. Stir until mixture is thoroughly blended (mixture will be soft). Spray cookie sheet with a vegetable-oil spray. Drop cookie dough onto the greased cookie sheet. Bake at 350°F (175°C) for 15 to 20 minutes. Move to cooling rack.

Yield: 24 cookies
Exchange, 1 cookie: ⅓ bread
Calories, 1 cookie: 26
Carbohydrates, 1 cookie: 4 g

Banana Date Cookies

1 small	very ripe banana	1 small
½ c.	low-fat cottage cheese	125 mL
3 T.	granulated sugar replacement	45 mL
2 T.	granulated fructose	30 mL
1 t.	vanilla extract	5 mL
1	egg	1
1⅓ c.	biscuit mix	340 mL
⅓ c.	chopped dates	90 mL

Beat banana and cottage cheese until creamy. (This can be done in a food processor.) Add sugar replacement, fructose, and vanilla extract. Beat well. Beat in egg. Beat in biscuit mix, ⅓ c. (90 mL) at a time. (Beat well after each addition.) Fold in chopped dates. Allow cookie dough to rest 5 minutes before dropping onto cookie sheet. Adjust oven rack to upper half. Spray cookie sheet with a vegetable-oil spray. Drop cookie dough onto the greased cookie sheet. Bake at 375°F (190°C) for 12 to 15 minutes or until lightly browned. Move cookies to cooling rack immediately.

Yield: 36 cookies
Exchange, 1 cookie: ⅓ bread
Calories, 1 cookie: 29
Carbohydrates, 1 cookie: 5 g

Bran Cookies

½ c.	100% bran cereal	125 mL
¼ c.	skim milk	60 mL
1 T.	margarine	15 mL
1	egg white	1
1 T.	granulated sugar replacement	15 mL
1 T.	granulated fructose	15 mL
1 t.	vanilla extract	5 mL
¾ c.	all-purpose flour	190 mL
1 t.	baking powder	5 mL

Combine bran cereal and skim milk in a medium-size microwave bowl. Cover with paper towels, and cook in the microwave on HIGH for 1½ minutes. Stir in margarine until melted. Set aside to cool slightly. Add egg white, sugar replacement, fructose, and vanilla. Stir to blend thoroughly. Stir in flour and baking powder. Spray cookie sheet lightly with a vegetable-oil spray. Drop cookie dough onto the greased cookie sheet. Bake at 375°F (190°C) for 10 to 12 minutes. Remove from cookie sheet, and cool on rack.

Yield: 24 cookies
Exchange, 1 cookie: ⅓ bread
Calories, 1 cookie: 29
Carbohydrates, 1 cookie: 4 g

Raisin Bran Cookies

⅓ c.	raisins	90 mL
½ c.	water	125 mL
½ c.	100% bran cereal	125 mL
1 T.	margarine	15 mL
½ t.	brandy flavoring	2 mL
½ t.	vanilla extract	2 mL
1	egg white	1
2 T.	granulated sugar replacement	30 mL
1 c.	all-purpose flour	250 mL
1 t.	baking powder	5 mL
2 t.	aspartame sweetener	10 mL

Combine raisins and water in a medium-size microwave bowl. Cover with paper towels, and cook in the microwave on HIGH for 5 minutes. Stir in bran cereal, margarine, brandy flavoring, and vanilla. Cover with paper towels, and set aside for 3 to 5 minutes, or until bran is soft. Place egg white in a small bowl or cup, and beat with a wire whisk until frothy. Add egg white and sugar replacement to cookie dough. Stir to thoroughly mix. Add flour and baking powder. Stir to blend completely. Spray cookie sheets lightly with a vegetable-oil spray. Drop cookie dough onto the greased cookie sheets. Flatten slightly, either with your fingers or the knife used for dropping the dough. Bake at 375°F (190°C) for 10 to 12 minutes. Remove from cookie sheets, and cool on racks. Sprinkle warm (not hot) cookies with aspartame sweetener.

Yield: 30 cookies
Exchange, 1 cookie: ⅓ bread
Calories, 1 cookie: 26
Carbohydrates, 1 cookie: 4 g

Banana Bran Cookies

½ c.	100% bran cereal	125 mL
¼ c.	water	60 mL
1 T.	margarine	15 mL
2 small	very ripe bananas, mashed	2 small
1 t.	vanilla extract	5 mL
1 T.	powdered butter flavoring	15 mL
1	egg white	1
2 T.	granulated sugar replacement	30 mL
1 c.	all-purpose flour	250 mL
1 t.	baking powder	5 mL

Combine bran cereal and water in a medium-size microwave bowl. Cover with paper towels, and cook in the microwave on HIGH for 1½ minutes. Stir in margarine, mashed banana, and vanilla. Cover with paper towels, and set aside for 3 to 5 minutes to allow flavors to mingle. Stir in butter flavoring and egg white. Add sugar replacement, flour, and baking powder. Stir to blend completely. Spray cookie sheets lightly with a vegetable-oil spray. Drop cookie dough onto the greased cookie sheets. Flatten slightly, either with your fingers or the knife used for dropping the dough. Bake at 375°F (190°C) for 10 to 12 minutes. Remove from cookie sheets, and cool on racks.

Yield: 30 cookies
Exchange, 1 cookie: ⅓ bread
Calories, 1 cookie: 28
Carbohydrates, 1 cookie: 4 g

Cranberry Walnut Bran Cookies

½ c.	100% bran cereal	125 mL
¼ c.	water	60 mL
1 T.	margarine	15 mL
1	egg white	1
2 T.	granulated sugar replacement	30 mL
1 T.	granulated fructose	15 mL
1 t.	vanilla extract	5 mL
¼ c.	chopped cranberries	60 mL
2 T.	chopped walnuts	30 mL
½ c. + 2 T.	all-purpose flour	155 mL
1 t.	baking powder	5 mL

Combine bran cereal and water in a medium-size microwave bowl. Cover with paper towels, and cook in the microwave on HIGH for 1½ minutes. Stir in margarine until melted. Set aside to cool slightly. Add egg white, sugar replacement, fructose, and vanilla. Stir to blend thoroughly. Blend in cranberries and walnuts. Add flour and baking powder. Stir to blend completely. Spray cookie sheet lightly with a vegetable-oil spray. Drop cookie dough onto the greased cookie sheet. Bake at 375°F (190°C) for 10 to 12 minutes. Remove from cookie sheet, and cool on rack.

Yield: 24 cookies
Exchange, 1 cookie: ⅓ bread
Calories, 1 cookie: 22
Carbohydrates, 1 cookie: 3 g

Pineapple Wheat Cookies

8-oz. can	crushed pineapple in juice	224-g can
½ c.	natural wheat & barley cereal (Grape-Nuts®)	125 mL
1 T.	margarine	15 mL
1 t.	pineapple flavoring	5 mL
1	egg white	1
1 T.	granulated fructose	15 mL
1 T.	granulated sugar replacement	15 mL
1 c.	all-purpose flour	250 mL
1 t.	baking powder	5 mL

Combine crushed pineapple in juice with cereal in a medium-size microwave bowl. Cover with paper towels. Microwave on HIGH for 2 to 3 minutes. Stir in margarine, re-cover, and allow to cool for 5 minutes. Add pineapple flavoring, egg white, fructose, and sugar replacement. Beat with a fork to blend completely. Stir in flour and baking powder thoroughly. Spray cookie sheets lightly with a vegetable-oil spray. Drop cookie dough onto the greased cookie sheets. Flatten slightly, either with your fingers or the knife used for dropping the dough. Bake at 375°F (190°C) for 12 to 15 minutes. Remove from cookie sheets, and cool on racks.

Yield: 30 cookies
Exchange, 1 cookie: ¼ bread
Calories, 1 cookie: 23
Carbohydrates, 1 cookie: 3 g

Walnut Wheat Drops

⅓ c.	skim milk	90 mL
½ c.	natural wheat & barley cereal (Grape-Nuts®)	125 mL
1 T.	margarine	15 mL
1 t.	vanilla extract	5 mL
1 t.	burnt-sugar flavoring	5 mL
1	egg white	1
1 T.	granulated fructose	15 mL
1 T.	granulated sugar replacement	15 mL
¼ c.	finely ground walnuts	60 mL
1 c.	all-purpose flour	250 mL
1 t.	baking powder	5 mL

Combine milk and cereal in a medium-size microwave bowl. Cover with paper towels. Microwave on HIGH for 2 to 3 minutes. Stir in margarine, re-cover, and allow to cool for 5 minutes. Add vanilla, burnt-sugar flavoring, egg white, fructose, and sugar replacement. Beat with a fork to blend completely. Stir in walnuts, and allow to rest for 2 minutes. Thoroughly stir in flour and baking powder. Spray cookie sheets lightly with a vegetable-oil spray. Drop cookie dough onto the greased cookie sheets. Bake at 375°F (190°C) for 12 to 15 minutes. Remove from cookie sheets, and cool on racks.

Yield: 30 cookies
Exchange, 1 cookie: ⅓ bread
Calories, 1 cookie: 26
Carbohydrates, 1 cookie: 4 g

Butter Pecan Wheat Cookies

⅓ c.	low-fat milk	90 mL
½ c.	natural wheat & barley cereal (Grape-Nuts®)	125 mL
1 T.	margarine	15 mL
1 T.	powdered butter flavoring	15 mL
1 t.	vanilla extract	5 mL
1	egg	1
1 T.	granulated fructose	15 mL
2 T.	granulated sugar replacement	30 mL
¼ c.	finely ground pecans	60 mL
1 c.	all-purpose flour	250 mL
1 t.	baking powder	5 mL

Combine milk and cereal in a medium-size microwave bowl. Cover with paper towels. Microwave on HIGH for 2 to 3 minutes. Stir in margarine and butter flavoring, re-cover, and allow to cool for 5 minutes. Add vanilla, egg, fructose, and sugar replacement. Beat with a fork to blend completely. Stir in pecans. Thoroughly stir in flour and baking powder. Spray cookie sheets lightly with a vegetable-oil spray. Drop cookie dough onto the greased cookie sheets. Flatten dough slightly, either with your fingers or the knife used for dropping the dough. Bake at 375°F (190°C) for 12 to 15 minutes. Remove from cookie sheets, and cool on racks.

Yield: 30 cookies
Exchange, 1 cookie: ⅓ bread
Calories, 1 cookie: 29
Carbohydrates, 1 cookie: 5 g

Cranberry Wheat Cookies

½ c.	cranberry juice	125 mL
½ c.	natural wheat & barley cereal (Grape-Nuts®)	125 mL
1 T.	margarine	15 mL
1 t.	vanilla extract	5 mL
1	egg white	1
2 T.	granulated fructose	30 mL
1 T.	granulated sugar replacement	15 mL
1 c.	all-purpose flour	250 mL
1 t.	baking powder	5 mL

Combine cranberry juice and cereal in a medium-size microwave bowl. Cover with paper towels. Microwave on HIGH for 2 to 3 minutes. Stir in margarine, re-cover, and allow to cool for 5 minutes. Add vanilla, egg white, fructose, and sugar replacement. Beat with a fork to blend completely. Thoroughly stir in flour and baking powder. Spray cookie sheets lightly with a vegetable-oil spray. Drop cookie dough onto the greased cookie sheets. Flatten dough slightly, either with your fingers or the knife used for dropping the dough. Bake at 375°F (190°C) for 12 to 15 minutes. Remove from cookie sheets, and cool on racks.

Yield: 30 cookies
Exchange, 1 cookie: ⅓ bread
Calories, 1 cookie: 20
Carbohydrates, 1 cookie: 5 g

Spicy Wheat Cookies

½ c.	water	125 mL
3 in.	cinnamon stick	7.5 cm
½ t.	allspice	2 mL
½ c.	natural wheat & barley cereal (Grape-Nuts®)	125 mL
1 T.	margarine	15 mL
1	egg	1
2 T.	granulated sugar replacement	30 mL
½ c.	all-purpose flour	125 mL
½ t.	baking powder	2 mL

Combine water, cinnamon stick, and allspice in a small saucepan. Boil for 2 minutes. Stir in cereal. Cover and allow to rest 3 minutes. Remove cinnamon stick. Thoroughly stir in margarine, egg, and sugar replacement. Stir and completely work in flour and baking powder. Spray cookie sheet lightly with a vegetable-oil spray. Drop cookie dough onto the greased cookie sheet. If desired, flatten dough slightly, either with your fingers or the knife used for dropping the dough. Bake at 375°F (190°C) for 12 to 15 minutes. Remove from cookie sheet, and cool on rack.

Yield: 24 cookies
Exchange, 1 cookie: ¼ bread
Calories, 1 cookie: 20
Carbohydrates, 1 cookie: 3 g

Soft Chocolate Cookies

½ c.	cold, diluted tomato soup	125 mL
½ c.	semisweet chocolate chips	125 mL
1	egg white	1
⅓ c.	granulated fructose	90 mL
1 t.	vanilla extract	5 mL
1 t.	chocolate flavoring	5 mL
1½ c.	all-purpose flour	375 mL
1½ t.	baking powder	7 mL
2 t.	aspartame sweetener	10 mL

Combine the tomato soup and ¼ c. (60 mL) of the chocolate chips in a small saucepan. Melt the chocolate chips in the tomato soup over low heat. Cool. Add egg white, and stir vigorously until well mixed. Blend in fructose, vanilla extract, and chocolate flavoring. Add ¾ c. (190 mL) flour, and beat until mixture is smooth. Stir in remaining flour, baking powder, and the remaining ¼ c. (60 mL) chocolate chips. Spray cookie sheets with a vegetable-oil spray. Drop small mounds of cookie dough onto the greased cookie sheets. Bake at 350°F (175°C) for 15 minutes. Immediately transfer to plate or breadboard; then sprinkle lightly with aspartame sweetener.

Yield: 42 cookies
Exchange, 1 cookie: ⅓ bread
Calories, 1 cookie: 25
Carbohydrates, 1 cookie: 3 g

Triple-Juice Cookies

¼ c.	pineapple juice	60 mL
¼ c.	orange juice	60 mL
2 T.	lemon juice	30 mL
½ c.	natural wheat & barley cereal (Grape-Nuts®)	125 mL
1 T.	margarine	15 mL
1 t.	vanilla extract	5 mL
2	egg whites	2
1 T.	granulated sugar replacement	15 mL
½ c.	all-purpose flour	125 mL
½ t.	baking powder	2 mL

Combine pineapple, orange, and lemon juice in a small saucepan. Bring to boil, and boil until liquid measures ⅓ c. (90 mL). Stir in cereal and margarine. Cover with paper towels, and allow to cool. Add vanilla, egg whites, and sugar replacement. Beat with a fork to blend completely. Thoroughly stir in flour and baking powder. Spray cookie sheet lightly with a vegetable-oil spray. Drop cookie dough onto the greased cookie sheet. Flatten dough slightly, either with your fingers or the knife used for dropping the dough. Bake at 375°F (190°C) for 12 to 15 minutes. Remove from cookie sheet, and cool on rack.

Yield: 24 cookies
Exchange, 1 cookie: ¼ bread
Calories, 1 cookie: 23
Carbohydrates, 1 cookie: 3 g

Pink & Pretty Cookies

¾ c.	cold, diluted tomato soup	190 mL
1	egg	1
⅓ c.	granulated fructose	90 mL
1 t.	vanilla extract	5 mL
1½ c.	all-purpose flour	375 mL
1½ t.	baking powder	7 mL
2 t.	aspartame sweetener	10 mL

Combine the tomato soup and egg in a medium-size bowl. Beat or stir vigorously until well mixed. Blend in fructose and vanilla. Add ¾ c. (190 mL) flour, and beat until mixture is smooth. Stir in remaining flour and baking powder. Spray cookie sheets with a vegetable-oil spray. Drop small mounds of cookie dough onto the greased cookie sheets. Bake at 350°F (175°C) for 15 minutes. Immediately transfer to plate or breadboard; then sprinkle lightly with aspartame sweetener.

Yield: 42 cookies
Exchange, 1 cookie: ¼ bread
Calories, 1 cookie: 20
Carbohydrates, 1 cookie: 3 g

Cocoa Pretty Cookies

¾ c.	cold, diluted tomato soup	190 mL
1	egg	1
⅓ c.	granulated fructose	90 mL
1 t.	vanilla extract	5 mL
¼ c.	cocoa powder	60 mL
1¼ c.	all-purpose flour	310 mL
1½ t.	baking powder	7 mL
2 t.	aspartame sweetener	10 mL

Combine the tomato soup and egg in a medium-size bowl. Beat or stir vigorously until well mixed. Blend in fructose and vanilla. Add cocoa powder and ¼ c. (60 mL) flour, and beat until mixture is smooth. Stir in remaining flour and baking powder. Spray cookie sheet with a vegetable-oil spray. Drop small mounds of cookie dough onto the greased cookie sheet. Bake at 350°F (175°C) for 15 minutes. Immediately transfer to plate or breadboard; then sprinkle lightly with aspartame sweetener.

Yield: 36 cookies
Exchange, 1 cookie: ¼ bread
Calories, 1 cookie: 20
Carbohydrates, 1 cookie: 3 g

Fig Cookies

8-oz. box	white cake mix, fructose-sweetened	227-g box
3 T	warm water	45 mL
¼ c.	dried brown figs*	60 mL
1 T.	liquid fructose	15 mL

*Although the figs are "dried," they should be soft and moist; don't use them if they are hard and dry.

Combine cake mix, warm water, figs, and liquid fructose in a medium-size bowl. Using a kitchen fork, stir to blend completely. Drop on a cool, greased cookie sheet. Bake at 375°F (190°C) for 12 to 15 minutes or until golden brown. Move to cooling rack.

Yield: 24 cookies
Exchange, 1 cookie: ½ bread, ¼ fat
Calories, 1 cookie: 49
Carbohydrates, 1 cookie: 8 g

Maple Cookies

8-oz. box	white cake mix, fructose-sweetened	227-g box
1	egg white	1
2 T.	dietetic maple syrup	30 mL
½ t.	maple flavoring	1 mL

Combine cake mix, egg white, maple syrup, and maple flavoring in a medium-size bowl. Stir to blend completely. Drop on a cool, greased cookie sheet. Bake at 375°F (190°C) for 12 to 15 minutes or until golden brown. Move to cooling rack.

Yield: 24 cookies
Exchange, 1 cookie: ⅓ bread, ¼ fat
Calories, 1 cookie: 48
Carbohydrates, 1 cookie: 5 g

Sweet & Nutty Cookies

¾ c.	cold, diluted tomato soup	190 mL
1	egg white	1
⅓ c.	granulated fructose	90 mL
1 t.	vanilla extract	5 mL
1½ c.	all-purpose flour	375 mL
¼ c.	finely chopped pecans	60 mL
1½ t.	baking powder	7 mL
2 t.	aspartame sweetener	10 mL

Combine the tomato soup and egg white in a medium-size bowl. Beat or stir vigorously until well mixed. Blend in fructose and vanilla. Add ¾ c. (190 mL) flour, and beat until mixture is smooth. Stir in chopped pecans. Stir in remaining flour and baking powder. Spray cookie sheets with a vegetable-oil spray. Drop small mounds of cookie dough onto the greased cookie sheets. Bake at 350°F (175°C) for 15 minutes. Immediately transfer to plate or breadboard; then sprinkle lightly with aspartame sweetener.

Yield: 42 cookies
Exchange, 1 cookie: ⅓ bread
Calories, 1 cookie: 24
Carbohydrates, 1 cookie: 3 g

Cherry-Pink Cookies

¾ c.	cold, diluted tomato soup	190 mL
1	egg	1
⅓ c.	granulated fructose	90 mL
1 t.	vanilla extract	5 mL
1½ c.	all-purpose flour	375 mL
½ c.	frozen sweet cherries, chopped	125 mL
1½ t.	baking powder	7 mL
2 t.	aspartame sweetener	10 mL

Combine the tomato soup and egg in a medium-size bowl. Beat or stir vigorously until well mixed. Blend in fructose and vanilla. Add ¾ c. (190 mL) flour, and beat until mixture is smooth. Stir in chopped cherries. Stir in remaining flour and baking powder. Spray cookie sheet with a vegetable-oil spray. Drop small mounds of cookie dough onto the greased cookie sheet. Bake at 350°F (175°C) for 15 minutes. Immediately transfer to plate or breadboard; then sprinkle lightly with aspartame sweetener.

Yield: 42 cookies
Exchange, 1 cookie: 1/3 bread
Calories, 1 cookie: 23
Carbohydrates, 1 cookie: 3 g

Walnut Chocolate-Chip Cookies

8-oz. box	white cake mix, fructose-sweetened	227-g box
1	egg	1
1 T.	caramel flavoring	15 mL
1/4 c.	chopped walnuts	60 mL
1/4 c.	mini chocolate chips	60 mL

Combine cake mix, egg, and caramel flavoring in a medium-size bowl. Stir to blend completely. Stir in walnuts and chocolate chips. Drop on a cool, greased cookie sheet. Bake at 375°F (190°C) for 12 to 15 minutes or until golden brown. Move to cooling rack.

Yield: 24 cookies
Exchange, 1 cookie: 1/3 bread, 1/2 fat
Calories, 1 cookie: 54
Carbohydrates, 1 cookie: 5 g

Almond Fancies

8-oz. box	white cake mix, fructose-sweetened	227-g box
1/3 c.	blanched almonds, finely chopped	90 mL
1	egg white	1
3 T.	warm water	45 mL

Combine cake mix, almonds, egg white, and water in a medium-size bowl. Using a kitchen fork, stir to blend completely. Drop on a cool, greased cookie sheet. Bake at 375°F (190°C) for 12 to 15 minutes or until golden brown. Move to cooling rack.

Yield: 24 cookies
Exchange, 1 cookie: 1/3 bread, 1/4 fat
Calories, 1 cookie: 52
Carbohydrates, 1 cookie: 5 g

Malted-Milk Cookies

8-oz. box	yellow cake mix, fructose-sweetened	227-g box
¼ c.	instant malted-milk powder	60 mL
1	egg	1
2 T.	water	30 mL

Combine cake mix, malted-milk powder, egg, and water in a medium-size bowl. Stir to blend completely. Drop on a cool, greased cookie sheet. Bake at 375°F (190°C) for 12 to 15 minutes or until golden brown. Move to cooling rack.

Yield: 24 cookies
Exchange, 1 cookie: ⅓ bread, ¼ fat
Calories, 1 cookie: 47
Carbohydrates, 1 cookie: 5 g

Easy Cranberry Cookies

8-oz. box	white cake mix, fructose-sweetened	227-g box
1	egg white	1
2 T.	water	30 mL
⅓ c.	chopped fresh cranberries	90 mL
½ t.	vanilla extract	2 mL

Combine cake mix, egg white, water, chopped cranberries, and vanilla extract in a medium-size bowl. Stir to blend completely. Drop on a cool, greased cookie sheet. Bake at 375°F (190°C) for 12 to 15 minutes or until golden brown. Move to cooling rack.

Yield: 24 cookies
Exchange, 1 cookie: ⅓ bread, ¼ fat
Calories, 1 cookie: 46
Carbohydrates, 1 cookie: 4 g

Plum Spice Cookies

6-oz. jar	baby-food plum purée	170-g jar
¼ c.	frozen orange-juice concentrate	60 mL
2 T.	granulated sugar replacement	30 mL

1	egg, slightly beaten	1
1 t.	vanilla extract	5 mL
¾ t.	allspice	3 mL
1 c.	all-purpose flour	250 mL
1 t.	baking powder	5 mL

Combine plum purée, orange-juice concentrate, and sugar replacement in a medium-size bowl. Stir to blend completely. Add egg and vanilla. Beat to mix. Add allspice, flour, and baking powder. Stir until mixture is thoroughly blended (mixture will be soft). Spray cookie sheet with a vegetable-oil spray. Drop cookie dough onto the greased cookie sheet. Bake at 350°F (175°C) for 15 to 20 minutes. Move to cooling racks.

Yield: 30 cookies
Exchange, 1 cookie: ⅓ bread
Calories, 1 cookie: 20
Carbohydrates, 1 cookie: 4 g

Plum Nutty Cookies

6-oz. jar	baby-food plum purée	170-g jar
¼ c.	frozen white grape-juice concentrate	60 mL
1 T.	granulated sugar replacement	15 mL
1	egg white	1
1 t.	vanilla extract	5 mL
1¼ c.	all-purpose flour	310 mL
1 t.	baking powder	5 mL
⅓ c.	finely ground walnuts	90 mL

Combine plum purée, grape-juice concentrate, and sugar replacement in a medium-size bowl. Stir to blend completely. Add egg white and vanilla. Beat to mix. Add flour and baking powder. Stir until mixture is thoroughly blended. Stir in ground walnuts. Spray cookie sheet with a vegetable-oil spray. Drop cookie dough onto the greased cookie sheet. Bake at 350°F (175°C) for 15 to 20 minutes. Move to cooling racks.

Yield: 30 cookies
Exchange, 1 cookie: ⅓ bread, ¼ fat
Calories, 1 cookie: 30
Carbohydrates, 1 cookie: 3 g

Apricot Raisin Cookies

6-oz. jar	baby-food apricot purée	170-g jar
¼ c.	frozen white grape-juice concentrate	60 mL
1 T.	granulated fructose	15 mL
1	egg white	1
1 t.	vanilla extract	5 mL
1¼ c.	all-purpose flour	310 mL
1 t.	baking powder	5 mL
⅓ c.	raisins, chopped	90 mL

Combine apricot purée, grape-juice concentrate, and fructose in a medium-size bowl. Stir to blend completely. Add egg white and vanilla. Beat to mix. Blend in flour and baking powder. Stir in chopped raisins. Spray cookie sheet with a vegetable-oil spray. Drop cookie dough onto the greased cookie sheet. Bake at 350°F (175°C) for 15 to 20 minutes. Move to cooling racks.

Yield: 30 cookies
Exchange, 1 cookie: ⅓ bread
Calories, 1 cookie: 27
Carbohydrates, 1 cookie: 4 g

Cottage Cheese with Currants Cookies

½ c.	nonfat cottage cheese	125 mL
¼ c.	granulated fructose	60 mL
1 T.	granulated sugar replacement	15 mL
1	egg white	1
1 t.	brandy flavoring	5 mL
¼ c.	currants	60 mL
¾ c.	all-purpose flour	190 mL

Combine cottage cheese, fructose, sugar replacement, egg white, and brandy flavoring in a medium-size mixing bowl. Beat to blend and so that cottage cheese breaks down into smaller pieces. Toss currants with ¼ c. (60 mL) of the flour to separate the currants. Add currants to cottage-cheese mixture, and stir to mix. Stir remaining ½ c. (125 mL) flour into mixture completely. Spray cookie sheet with a vegetable-oil spray. Drop cookie dough onto the greased cookie sheet. Bake at 350°F (175°C) for 12 to 15 minutes. Move to cooling rack.

Yield: 24 cookies
Exchange, 1 cookie: ¼ bread, ¼ fruit

Calories, 1 cookie: 33
Carbohydrates, 1 cookie: 7 g

Cottage-Cheese White Cookies

½ c.	nonfat cottage cheese	125 mL
¼ c.	granulated fructose	60 mL
1 T.	granulated sugar replacement	15 mL
1	egg white	1
1 t.	clear vanilla flavoring	5 mL
¾ c.	all-purpose flour	190 mL

Combine cottage cheese, fructose, sugar replacement, egg white, and vanilla in a medium-size mixing bowl. Beat to blend and so that cottage
cheese breaks down into smaller pieces. Stir in flour completely. Spray
cookie sheet with a vegetable-oil spray. Drop cookie dough onto the
greased cookie sheet. Bake at 350°F (175°C) for 12 to 15 minutes. Move
to cooling rack.

Yield: 24 cookies
Exchange, 1 cookie: ⅓ bread
Calories, 1 cookie: 26
Carbohydrates, 1 cookie: 4 g

Cream Cookies

8-oz. box	white cake mix, fructose-sweetened	227-g box
2 T.	whipping cream (heavy cream)	30 mL
1	egg white	1
1 T.	granulated sugar replacement	15 mL

Combine cake mix, whipping cream, egg white, and sugar replacement
in a medium-size bowl. Stir to blend completely. Drop on a cool, greased
cookie sheet. Bake at 375°F (190°C) for 12 to 15 minutes or until golden
brown. Move to cooling rack.

Yield: 24 cookies
Exchange, 1 cookie: ⅓ bread, ⅓ fat
Calories, 1 cookie: 46
Carbohydrates, 1 cookie: 5 g

Apple-Pie Cottage-Cheese Cookies

½ c.	nonfat cottage cheese	125 mL
¼ c.	granulated fructose	60 mL
1 T.	granulated sugar replacement	15 mL
1	egg white	1
1 t.	vanilla extract	5 mL
1 t.	apple-pie spices	5 mL
⅓ c.	finely chopped Delicious apple	90 mL
¾ c.	all-purpose flour	190 mL

Combine cottage cheese, fructose, sugar replacement, egg white, vanilla, and apple-pie spices in a medium-size mixing bowl. Beat to blend and so that cottage cheese breaks down into smaller pieces. Stir in chopped apple. Blend in flour completely. Spray cookie sheet with a vegetable-oil spray. Drop cookie dough onto the greased cookie sheet. Bake at 350°F (175°C) for 12 to 15 minutes. Move to cooling rack.

Yield: 24 cookies
Exchange, 1 cookie: ⅓ bread
Calories, 1 cookie: 31
Carbohydrates, 1 cookie: 5 g

Cottage-Cheese Chocolate Cookies

2¾ c.	all-purpose flour	690 mL
½ c.	baking cocoa	125 mL
1 t.	baking soda	5 mL
1 t.	baking powder	5 mL
½ t.	salt	2 mL
1 c.	margarine	250 mL
¾ c.	granulated sugar replacement	190 mL
½ c.	granulated fructose	125 mL
1 c.	small-curd low-fat cottage cheese	250 mL
2	eggs	2
2 t.	vanilla extract	10 mL

Sift flour, cocoa, baking soda, baking powder, and salt together twice. Set aside. Using an electric mixer, cream margarine, sugar replacement, and fructose. Beat in cottage cheese, eggs, and vanilla extract. Gradually beat in sifted dry ingredients. Beat well, Drop mixture on ungreased cookie sheet. Bake at 350°F (175°C) for 10 to 12 minutes or until no imprint remains when the cookie is pressed lightly with a finger. Move cookies to cooling racks.

Yield: 72 cookies
Exchange, 1 cookie: ⅓ bread, ¼ fat
Calories, 1 cookie: 38
Carbohydrates, 1 cookie: 4 g

Simple Anise Cookies

8-oz. box	white cake mix, fructose-sweetened	227-g box
1	egg	1
1 T.	water	15 mL
1 t.	anise seeds, crushed	5 mL

Combine cake mix, egg, water, and crushed anise seeds in a medium-size bowl. Using a kitchen fork, stir to blend completely. Drop on a cool, greased cookie sheet. Bake at 375°F (190°C) for 12 to 15 minutes or until golden brown. Move to cooling rack.

Yield: 24 cookies
Exchange, 1 cookie: ½ bread
Calories, 1 cookie: 45
Carbohydrates, 1 cookie: 6 g

Strawberry-Preserve Cookies

¼ c.	all-fruit strawberry preserves	60 mL
	warm water	
2 to 3 drops	red food coloring	2 to 3 drops
8-oz. box	white cake mix, fructose-sweetened	227-g box

Combine the strawberry preserves with enough warm water to make ⅓ c. (90 mL) of liquid. Stir in food coloring. Combine cake mix and strawberry mixture in a medium-size bowl. Stir to blend completely. (Mix will seem sticky.) Drop on a cool, greased cookie sheet. Bake at 375°F (190°C) for 12 to 15 minutes or until golden brown. Move to cooling rack.

Yield: 24 cookies
Exchange, 1 cookie: ½ bread
Calories, 1 cookie: 46
Carbohydrates, 1 cookie: 7 g

Banana Chocolate Cookies

1 small	very ripe banana	1 small
½ c.	low-fat cottage cheese	125 mL
3 T.	granulated sugar replacement	45 mL
2 T.	granulated fructose	30 mL
1 t.	vanilla extract	5 mL
1	egg	1
1⅓ c.	biscuit mix	340 mL
⅓ c.	chocolate chips	90 mL

Beat banana and cottage cheese until creamy. (This can be done in a food processor.) Add sugar replacement, fructose, and vanilla extract. Beat well. Beat in egg. Beat in biscuit mix, ⅓ c. (90 mL) at a time. (Beat well after each addition.) Place chocolate chips on cutting board and chop into small pieces; fold into cookie batter. Allow cookie dough to rest 5 minutes before dropping dough onto cookie sheet. Adjust oven rack to upper half. Spray cookie sheet with a vegetable-oil spray. Drop cookie dough onto the greased cookie sheet. Bake at 375°F (190°C) for 12 to 15 minutes or until lightly browned. Move cookies to cooling rack immediately.

Yield: 36 cookies
Exchange, 1 cookie: ⅓ bread
Calories, 1 cookie: 31
Carbohydrates, 1 cookie: 6 g

Chocolate Banana Pecan Cookies

8-oz. box	chocolate cake mix, fructose-sweetened	227-g box
⅓ c.	mashed banana*	90 mL
1	egg white	1
⅓ c.	chopped pecans	90 mL

*This is about half of a large banana.

Combine cake mix, mashed banana, and egg white in a medium-size bowl. Stir to blend completely. (Mix will seem sticky.) Stir in pecans. Drop on a cool, greased cookie sheet. Bake at 375°F (190°C) for 12 to 15 minutes or until golden brown. Move to cooling rack.

Yield: 24 cookies
Exchange, 1 cookie: ½ bread, ½ fat
Calories, 1 cookie: 56
Carbohydrates, 1 cookie: 8 g

Brandy Pecan Cookies

8-oz. box	white cake mix, fructose-sweetened	227-g box
1	egg white	1
1 T.	brandy	15 mL
24	pecan halves	24

Combine cake mix, egg white, and brandy in a medium-size bowl. Stir to blend completely. Drop on a cool, greased cookie sheet. Press a pecan half into the top of each cookie. Bake at 375°F (190°C) for 12 to 15 minutes or until golden brown. Move to cooling rack.

Yield: 24 cookies
Exchange, 1 cookie: ⅓ bread, ¼ fat
Calories, 1 cookie: 50
Carbohydrates, 1 cookie: 5 g

Sour-Cream Cookies

2¾ c.	all-purpose flour	690 mL
1½ t.	baking powder	7 mL
½ t.	baking soda	2 mL
½ t.	salt	2 mL
¼ t.	ground nutmeg	1 mL
1 c.	margarine	250 mL
¾ c.	granulated sugar replacement	190 mL
¼ c.	granulated fructose	60 mL
2	eggs	2
½ c.	low-calorie dairy sour cream	125 mL
¼ t.	lemon extract	1 mL
3 T.	aspartame sweetener	45 mL

Sift together flour, baking powder, baking soda, salt, and nutmeg. Set aside. Using an electric mixer, cream together margarine, sugar replacement, and fructose. Add eggs, one at a time, beating well after each addition. Beat in sour cream and lemon extract. Drop mixture on greased cookie sheet. Bake at 375°F (190°C) for 8 to 10 minutes. Move cookies to cooling racks. Sprinkle cookies with aspartame sweetener.

Yield: 78 cookies
Exchange, 1 cookie: ⅓ bread, ½ fat
Calories, 1 cookie: 32
Carbohydrates, 1 cookie: 4 g

Coffee Cookies

⅓ c.	boiling water	90 mL
2 T.	instant-coffee powder	30 mL
8-oz. box	white cake mix, fructose-sweetened	227-g box

Dissolve the instant coffee in the boiling water; then allow to cool. Combine cake mix and coffee/water in a medium-size bowl. Stir to blend completely. (Mix will seem sticky.) Drop on a cool, greased cookie sheet. Bake at 375°F (190°C) for 12 to 15 minutes, or until golden brown. Move to cooling rack.

Yield: 24 cookies
Exchange, 1 cookie: ½ bread
Calories, 1 cookie: 41
Carbohydrates, 1 cookie: 6 g

Toasted-Almond Yogurt Drops

8 oz.	low-fat vanilla yogurt	224 g
2	egg whites	2
2 T.	granulated sugar replacement	30 mL
2 T.	granulated fructose	30 mL
1 t.	almond flavoring	5 mL
⅓ c.	toasted almonds, crushed*	90 mL
1¼ c.	all-purpose flour	310 mL
1 t.	baking powder	5 mL

*To toast almonds: Sauté almond slices over low heat in a nonstick skillet until slices are lightly browned. Don't add any oil or shortening.

Combine vanilla yogurt and egg whites in a mixing bowl. Beat until thoroughly blended, about 1 minute. Add sugar replacement, fructose, almond flavoring, toasted almonds, and ½ c. (125 mL) of the flour. Beat until smooth. Stir in remaining flour and baking powder. Spray cookie sheet with a vegetable-oil spray. Drop cookie dough onto the greased cookie sheet. Bake at 350°F (175°C) for 12 to 15 minutes. Move to cooling racks.

Yield: 30 cookies
Exchange, 1 cookie: ⅓ bread, ¼ fat
Calories, 1 cookie: 34
Carbohydrates, 1 cookie: 4 g

Cherry-Yogurt Drops

8 oz.	low-fat cherry yogurt	224 g
2	egg whites	2
2 T.	granulated sugar replacement	30 mL
2 T.	granulated fructose	30 mL
2 t.	cherry flavoring	10 mL
3 T.	all-fruit cherry preserves	45 mL
1¼ c.	all-purpose flour	310 mL
1 t.	baking powder	5 mL

Combine cherry yogurt and egg whites in a mixing bowl. Beat until thoroughly blended, about 1 minute. Add sugar replacement, fructose, cherry flavoring, cherry preserves, and ½ c. (125 mL) of the flour. Beat until smooth. Stir in remaining flour and baking powder. Spray cookie sheet with a vegetable-oil spray. Drop cookie dough onto the greased cookie sheet. Bake at 350°F (175°C) for 12 to 15 minutes. Move to cooling racks.

Yield: 30 cookies
Exchange, 1 cookie: ⅓ bread
Calories, 1 cookie: 28
Carbohydrates, 1 cookie: 5 g

Caraway Yogurt Cookies

8-oz. box	yellow cake mix, fructose-sweetened	227-g box
⅓ c.	plain yogurt	90 mL
½ t.	ground nutmeg	2 mL
½ t.	caraway seeds	2 mL

Combine cake mix and yogurt in a medium-size bowl. Stir to blend completely. (Mix will seem sticky.) Stir in nutmeg and caraway seeds. Drop on a cool, greased cookie sheet. Bake at 375°F (190°C) for 12 to 15 minutes or until golden brown. Move to cooling rack.

Yield: 24 cookies
Exchange, 1 cookie: ⅔ bread
Calories, 1 cookie: 42
Carbohydrates, 1 cookie: 7 g

Lemon-Yogurt Drops

8 oz.	low-fat lemon yogurt	224 g
2	egg whites	2
2 T.	granulated sugar replacement	30 mL
2 T.	granulated fructose	30 mL
2 T.	freshly grated lemon rind	30 mL
1¼ c.	all-purpose flour	310 mL
1 t.	baking powder	5 mL

Combine lemon yogurt and egg whites in a mixing bowl. Beat until thoroughly blended, about 1 minute. Add sugar replacement, fructose, lemon rind, and ½ c. (125 mL) of the flour. Beat until smooth. Stir in remaining flour and baking powder. Spray cookie sheet with a vegetable-oil spray. Drop cookie dough onto the greased cookie sheet. Bake at 350°F (175°C) for 12 to 15 minutes. Move to cooling racks.

Yield: 30 cookies
Exchange, 1 cookie: ⅓ bread
Calories, 1 cookie: 27
Carbohydrates, 1 cookie: 4 g

Rum Raisin Cookies

½ c.	raisins	125 mL
¼ c.	dark rum	60 mL
	water	
8-oz. box	yellow cake mix, fructose-sweetened	227-g box

Combine raisins and dark rum in a saucepan. Bring to a boil; then remove from heat and allow to cool. When cool, drain remaining rum liquid into a 1-c. (250-mL) measuring cup. Add enough water to make ⅓ c. (90 mL) of liquid. Combine cake mix and the ⅓ c. (90 mL) of rum liquid in a medium-size bowl. Stir to blend completely. (Mix will seem sticky.) Stir in raisins. Drop on a cool, greased cookie sheet. Bake at 375°F (190°C) for 12 to 15 minutes or until golden brown. Move to cooling rack.

Yield: 24 cookies
Exchange, 1 cookie: ¾ bread
Calories, 1 cookie: 54
Carbohydrates, 1 cookie: 12 g

Swedish Classic Cookies

8-oz. box	yellow cake mix, fructose-sweetened	227-g box
⅓ c.	water	90 mL
2 t.	liquid fructose	10 mL
1 t.	ground coriander seeds	5 mL
½ t.	ground cinnamon	2 mL

Combine cake mix, water, and liquid fructose in a medium-size bowl. Stir to blend completely. (Mix will seem sticky.) Stir in coriander seeds and cinnamon. Drop on a cool, greased cookie sheet. Bake at 375°F (190°C) for 12 to 15 minutes or until golden brown. Move to cooling rack.

Yield: 24 cookies
Exchange, 1 cookie: ⅔ bread
Calories, 1 cookie: 43
Carbohydrates, 1 cookie: 9 g

Whole-Wheat Cookies

1½ c.	whole-wheat flour	375 mL
1 t.	baking powder	5 mL
¼ t.	baking soda	1 mL
dash	salt	dash
1 c.	margarine	250 mL
⅔ c.	granulated sugar replacement	190 mL
⅓ c.	granulated fructose	90 mL
2	eggs	2
¼ c.	apple juice	60 mL

Combine whole-wheat flour, baking powder, baking soda, and salt in a sifter. Sift together into a bowl. Set aside. Using an electric mixer, cream margarine. Gradually add granulated sugar replacement and fructose. Add eggs, one at a time, beating well after each addition. Add flour mixture alternately with apple juice. Beat until smooth. Drop onto ungreased cookie sheets. Bake at 350°F (175°C) until edges are browned and top feels firm to the touch. Move to cooling racks.

Yield: 60 cookies
Exchange, 1 cookie: ¼ bread, ½ fat
Calories, 1 cookie: 41
Carbohydrates, 1 cookie: 3 g

Whole-Wheat Oatmeal Cookies

1½ c.	whole-wheat flour	375 mL
1 t.	baking powder	5 mL
¼ t.	baking soda	1 mL
dash	salt	dash
1 c.	margarine	250 mL
⅔ c.	granulated sugar replacement	190 mL
⅓ c.	granulated fructose	90 mL
2	eggs	2
¼ c.	apple juice	60 mL
1 c.	quick-cooking oatmeal	250 mL

Combine whole-wheat flour, baking powder, baking soda, and salt in a sifter. Sift together into a bowl. Set aside. Using an electric mixer, cream margarine. Gradually add granulated sugar replacement and fructose. Add eggs, one at a time, beating well after each addition. Add flour mixture alternately with apple juice. Beat until smooth. Stir in oatmeal. Drop onto ungreased cookie sheet. Bake at 350°F (175°C) until edges are browned and top feels firm to the touch. Move to cooling rack.

Yield: 60 cookies
Exchange, 1 cookie: ⅓ bread, ½ fat
Calories, 1 cookie: 49
Carbohydrates, 1 cookie: 5 g

Spice Whole-Wheat Cookies

1½ c.	whole-wheat flour	375 mL
1 t.	baking powder	5 mL
¼ t.	baking soda	1 mL
dash	salt	dash
2 t.	ground cinnamon	10 mL
1 t.	ground nutmeg	5 mL
¼ t.	ground cloves	1 mL
1 c.	margarine	250 mL
⅔ c.	granulated sugar replacement	190 mL
⅓ c.	granulated fructose	90 mL
2	eggs	2
¼ c.	white grape juice	60 mL

Combine whole-wheat flour, baking powder, baking soda, salt, cinnamon, nutmeg, and cloves in a sifter. Sift together into a bowl. Set aside. Using an electric mixer, cream margarine. Gradually add granulated sugar replacement and fructose. Add eggs, one at a time, beating well after each addition. Add flour mixture alternately with grape juice. Beat until smooth. Drop onto ungreased cookie sheet. Bake at 350°F (175°C) until edges are brown and top feels firm. Move to wire racks.

Yield: 60 cookies
Exchange, 1 cookie: ⅓ bread, ½ fat
Calories, 1 cookie: 46
Carbohydrates, 1 cookie: 4 g

Orange Whole-Wheat Cookies

1½ c.	whole-wheat flour	375 mL
1 t.	baking powder	5 mL
¼ t.	baking soda	1 mL
dash	salt	dash
1 c.	margarine	250 mL
⅔ c.	granulated sugar replacement	190 mL
⅓ c.	granulated fructose	90 mL
1 T.	fresh, grated orange rind	15 mL
2 t.	lemon peel	10 mL
2	eggs	2
¼ c.	orange-juice concentrate	60 mL

Combine whole-wheat flour, baking powder, baking soda, and salt in a sifter. Sift together into a bowl. Set aside. Using an electric mixer, cream margarine. Gradually add granulated sugar replacement and fructose. Beat in orange rind and lemon peel. Add eggs, one at a time, beating well after each addition. Add flour mixture alternately with orange-juice concentrate. Beat until smooth. Drop onto ungreased cookie sheet. Bake at 350°F (175°C) until edges are brown and top feels firm to the touch. Move to cooling racks.

Yield: 60 cookies
Exchange, 1 cookie: ⅓ bread, ½ fat
Calories, 1 cookie: 48
Carbohydrates, 1 cookie: 4 g

Salty-Peanut Whole-Wheat Cookies

1½ c.	whole-wheat flour	375 mL
1 t.	baking powder	5 mL
¼ t.	baking soda	1 mL
dash	salt	dash
1 c.	margarine	250 mL
⅔ c.	granulated sugar replacement	190 mL
⅓ c.	granulated fructose	90 mL
2	eggs	2
¼ c.	white grape juice	60 mL
⅓ c.	salted peanuts, chopped	90 mL

Combine whole-wheat flour, baking powder, baking soda, and salt in a sifter. Sift together into a bowl. Set aside. Using an electric mixer, cream margarine. Gradually add granulated sugar replacement and fructose. Add eggs, one at a time, beating well after each addition. Add flour mixture alternately with grape juice. Beat until smooth. Stir in chopped peanuts. Drop onto ungreased cookie sheet. Bake at 350°F (175°C) until edges are brown and top feels firm. Move to cooling racks.

Yield: 60 cookies
Exchange, 1 cookie: ⅓ bread, ½ fat
Calories, 1 cookie: 51
Carbohydrates, 1 cookie: 5 g

Apple Oatmeal Whole-Wheat Cookies

1½ c.	whole-wheat flour	250 mL
2 t.	apple-pie spices	10 mL
1 t.	baking powder	5 mL
¼ t.	baking soda	1 mL
dash	salt	dash
1 c.	quick-cooking oatmeal	250 mL
1 c.	margarine	250 mL
⅔ c.	granulated brown-sugar replacement	190 mL
⅓ c.	granulated fructose	90 mL
2	eggs	2
¼ c.	apple juice	60 mL
¼ c.	finely chopped apple	60 mL

Combine whole-wheat flour, apple-pie spices, baking powder, baking soda, and salt in a sifter. Stir in quick oatmeal. Sift together into a bowl. Set aside. Using an electric mixer, cream margarine. Gradually add granulated brown-sugar replacement and fructose. Add eggs, one at a time, beating well after each addition. Add flour mixture alternately with apple juice. Beat until smooth. Stir in chopped apple. Drop onto ungreased cookie sheet. Bake at 350°F (175°C) until edges are brown and top feels firm. Move to cooling racks.

Yield: 72 cookies
Exchange, 1 cookie: ¼ bread, ½ fat
Calories, 1 cookie: 43
Carbohydrates, 1 cookie: 3 g

Date Whole-Wheat Cookies

1½ c.	whole-wheat flour	375 mL
1 t.	baking powder	5 mL
¼ t.	baking soda	1 mL
dash	salt	dash
1 c.	margarine	250 mL
⅔ c.	granulated sugar replacement	190 mL
⅓ c.	granulated fructose	90 mL
2	eggs	2
¼ c.	white grape juice	60 mL
⅓ c.	finely chopped dates	90 mL

Combine whole-wheat flour, baking powder, baking soda, and salt in a sifter. Sift together into a bowl. Set aside. Using an electric mixer, cream margarine. Gradually add granulated sugar replacement and fructose. Add eggs, one at a time, beating well after each addition. Add flour mixture alternately with grape juice. Beat until smooth. Stir in finely chopped dates. Drop onto ungreased cookie sheet. Bake at 350°F (175°C) until edges are brown and top feels firm. Move to cooling racks.

Yield: 60 cookies
Exchange, 1 cookie: ½ bread, ½ fat
Calories, 1 cookie: 58
Carbohydrates, 1 cookie: 7 g

Pecan Whole-Wheat Drops

1 c.	whole-wheat flour	250 mL
½ c.	all-purpose flour	125 mL
1 t.	baking powder	5 mL
¼ t.	baking soda	1 mL
dash	salt	dash
1 c.	margarine	250 mL
⅔ c.	granulated brown-sugar replacement	190 mL
⅓ c.	granulated fructose	90 mL
2	eggs	2
¼ c.	white grape juice	60 mL
⅓ c.	chopped pecans	90 mL

Combine whole-wheat flour, all-purpose flour, baking powder, baking soda, and salt in a sifter. Sift together into a bowl. Set aside. Using an electric mixer, cream margarine. Gradually add granulated sugar replacement and fructose. Add eggs, one at a time, beating well after each addition. Add flour mixture alternately with grape juice. Beat until smooth. Stir in chopped pecans. Drop onto ungreased cookie sheet. Bake at 350°F (175°C) until edges are brown and top feels firm. Move to cooling racks.

Yield: 60 cookies
Exchange, 1 cookie: ⅓ bread, ½ fat
Calories, 1 cookie: 47
Carbohydrates, 1 cookie: 4 g

Chocolate-Chip Whole-Wheat Cookies

1 c.	whole-wheat flour	250 mL
1 t.	baking powder	5 mL
¼ t.	baking soda	1 mL
dash	salt	dash
1 c.	quick-cooking oatmeal	250 mL
1 c.	margarine	250 mL
1 c.	margarine	250 mL
⅔ c.	granulated sugar replacement	190 mL
⅓ c.	granulated fructose	90 mL
2	eggs	2

| ¼ c. | white grape juice | 60 mL |
| ½ c. | mini chocolate chips | 125 mL |

Combine whole-wheat flour, baking powder, baking soda, and salt in a sifter. Sift together into a bowl. Stir in quick oatmeal. Set aside. Using an electric mixer, cream margarine. Gradually add granulated sugar replacement and fructose. Add eggs, one at a time, beating well after each addition. Add flour mixture alternately with grape juice. Beat until smooth. Stir in chocolate chips. Drop onto ungreased cookie sheet. Bake at 350°F (175°C) until edges are brown and top feels firm to the touch. Move to cooling racks.

Yield: 60 cookies
Exchange, 1 cookie: ⅓ bread, ½ fat
Calories, 1 cookie: 48
Carbohydrates, 1 cookie: 4 g

Applesauce Granola Drops

1	egg	1
1 T.	vegetable oil	15 mL
½ c.	unsweetened applesauce	125 mL
1 T.	apple-juice concentrate	15 mL
1 c.	all-purpose flour	250 mL
¼ t.	baking powder	1 mL
½ t.	ground nutmeg	2 mL
1 c.	granola cereal	250 mL

Combine egg, vegetable oil, applesauce, and apple-juice concentrate in a large mixing bowl. Beat to blend thoroughly. Add flour, baking powder, and nutmeg. Beat until completely mixed. Stir in granola cereal. Grease cookie sheet with vegetable-oil spray. Drop cookie dough onto cookie sheet. Bake at 350°F (175°C) for 7 to 10 minutes or until firm. Remove from oven, and cool on racks.

Yield: 30 cookies
Exchange, 1 cookie: ⅓ bread, ¼ fat
Calories, 1 cookie: 37
Carbohydrates, 1 cookie: 3 g

Carob Oatmeal Drops

¼ c.	mashed banana	60 mL
3 T.	vegetable oil	45 mL
½ t.	vanilla extract	2 mL
1	egg	1
2 T.	skim milk	30 mL
¾ c.	all-purpose flour	190 mL
2 T.	carob powder	30 mL
⅛ t.	baking powder	½ mL
⅓ c.	quick-cooking oatmeal	90 mL

Combine banana, vegetable oil, vanilla, egg, and skim milk in a mixing bowl. Beat until creamy. Beat in flour, carob powder, and baking powder. Beat well. Stir in oatmeal. Grease cookie sheet with vegetable-oil spray. Drop cookie dough onto cookie sheet. Bake at 350°F (175°C) for 8 to 10 minutes or until just firm. Remove from oven, and cool on racks.

Yield: 30 cookies
Exchange, 1 cookie: ⅓ bread
Calories, 1 cookie: 27
Carbohydrates, 1 cookie: 4 g

Banana Carob-Chip Cookies

¼ c.	mashed banana	60 mL
¼ c.	vegetable oil	60 mL
1	egg	1
1 c.	all-purpose flour	250 mL
1 c.	quick-cooking oatmeal	250 mL
½ c.	carob chips	125 mL

Combine banana, vegetable oil, and egg in a mixing bowl. Beat thoroughly. Stir in flour, oatmeal, and carob chips. Blend well. Grease cookie sheet with vegetable-oil spray. Drop cookie dough onto cookie sheet. Bake at 350°F (175°C) for 10 to 12 minutes, or until cookies begin to brown around edges. Remove from oven, and cool on racks.

Yield: 36 cookies
Exchange, 1 cookie: ⅓ bread, ¼ fat
Calories, 1 cookie: 38
Carbohydrates, 1 cookie: 4 g

Frosted Orange Cookies

8-oz. box	pound-cake mix, fructose-sweetened	227-g box
⅔ c.	orange-juice concentrate	180 mL
3.6-oz. box	frosting mix, fructose-sweetened	104-g box
1 T.	margarine	15 mL
2 to 3 T.	finely grated orange rind	30 to 45 mL

Combine cake mix and ⅓ c. (90 mL) of the orange-juice concentrate in a medium-size bowl. Stir to blend completely. (Mix will seem sticky.) Drop on a cool, greased cookie sheet. Bake at 375°F (190°C) for 12 to 15 minutes or until golden brown. Move to cooling rack. Meanwhile, combine the frosting mix and remaining ⅓ c. (90 mL) of orange-juice concentrate in a saucepan. Stir to blend; then place saucepan over medium heat and continue stirring until mixture is very thick and pastelike. Remove from heat, and stir in the margarine. Cool completely before frosting cookies. Frost cookies; then sprinkle a small amount of finely grated orange rind on the top of each one.

Yield: 24 cookies
Exchange, 1 cookie: ¾ bread, ½ fat
Calories, 1 cookie: 96
Carbohydrates, 1 cookie: 12 g

Frosted Strawberry Cookies

8-oz. box	pound-cake mix, fructose-sweetened	227-g box
⅓ c.	fresh strawberries, mashed	90 mL
3.6-oz. box	frosting mix, fructose-sweetened	104-g box
2 to 3 drops	red food coloring	2 to 3 drops

Combine cake mix and mashed strawberries in a medium-size bowl. Stir to blend completely. (Mix will seem sticky.) Drop on a cool, greased cookie sheet. Bake at 375°F (190°C) for 12 to 15 minutes or until golden brown. Move to cooling rack. Meanwhile, prepare frosting mix for vanilla-flavored frosting, following directions on box. Tint frosting with red food coloring. Cool completely before frosting cookies.

Yield: 24 cookies
Exchange, 1 cookie: ¾ bread, ½ fat
Calories, 1 cookie: 87
Carbohydrates, 1 cookie: 10 g

Sweet-Squash Cookies

⅓ c.	vegetable oil	90 mL
1	egg	1
1 c.	mashed acorn squash	250 mL
1½ c.	all-purpose flour	375 mL
1 t.	baking powder	5 mL
1 t.	allspice	5 mL
dash	cinnamon	dash

Combine oil, egg, and squash in a mixing bowl. Beat until thoroughly blended. Add flour, baking powder, and allspice. Beat well. Grease cookie sheet with a vegetable-oil spray. Drop cookie dough onto cookie sheet. If desired, sprinkle each cookie with a small amount of cinnamon. Bake at 350°F (175°C) for 10 to 12 minutes. Remove from oven, and cool on racks.

Yield: 36 cookies
Exchange, 1 cookie: ½ bread, ¼ fat
Calories, 1 cookie: 42
Carbohydrates, 1 cookie: 7 g

Coconut Orange Cookies

1¾ c.	all-purpose flour	440 mL
¼ t.	baking soda	1 mL
¼ t.	salt	1 mL
½ c.	margarine	125 mL
⅔ c.	granulated sugar replacement	190 mL
2 T.	granulated fructose	30 mL
1	egg	1
½ t.	grated orange rind	2 mL
½ t.	grated lemon rind	2 mL
¼ c.	orange juice	60 mL
1 T.	lemon juice	15 mL
½ c.	unsweetened flaked coconut	125 mL

Sift together flour, baking soda, and salt. Set aside. Using an electric mixer, cream margarine, sugar replacement, and fructose. Beat in egg and grated orange and lemon rinds. Beat in dry ingredients alternately with juices. (Beat well after each addition.) Stir in coconut. Drop mixture onto greased cookie sheet. Bake at 350°F (175°C) for 12 to 14 minutes or until edges begin to lightly brown. Move cookies to cooling racks.

Yield: 48 cookies
Exchange, 1 cookie: ⅓ bread, ⅓ fat
Calories, 1 cookie: 41
Carbohydrates, 1 cookie: 4 g

Kitchen-Sink Whole-Wheat Cookies

1 c.	whole-wheat flour	250 mL
1 t.	baking powder	5 mL
¼ t.	baking soda	1 mL
dash	salt	dash
1 c.	quick-cooking oatmeal	250 mL
1 c.	margarine	250 mL
⅔ c.	granulated sugar replacement	190 mL
⅓ c.	granulated fructose	90 mL
2	eggs	2
¼ c.	white grape juice	60 mL
½ c.	dried unsweetened fruit, chopped	125 mL
⅓ c.	granola cereal	90 mL

Combine whole-wheat flour, baking powder, baking soda, and salt in a sifter. Sift together into a bowl. Stir in oatmeal. Set aside. Using an electric mixer, cream margarine. Gradually add granulated sugar replacement and fructose. Add eggs, one at a time, and beat well after each addition. Add flour mixture alternately with grape juice. Beat until smooth. Stir in dried fruit and granola. Drop onto ungreased cookie sheet. Bake at 350°F (175°C) until edges are brown and top feels firm. Move to wire racks.

Yield: 60 cookies
Exchange, 1 cookie: ½ bread, ½ fat
Calories, 1 cookie: 51
Carbohydrates, 1 cookie: 8 g

Lemon-Yogurt-Cake Cookies

8-oz. box	pound cake mix, fructose-sweetened	227-g box
⅓ c.	low-fat lemon yogurt	90 mL
2 t.	freshly grated lemon rind	10 mL

Combine cake mix, lemon yogurt, and lemon rind in a medium-size bowl. Stir to blend completely. (Mix will seem sticky.) Drop on a cool, greased cookie sheet. Bake at 375°F (190°C) for 12 to 15 minutes or until golden brown. Move to cooling rack.

Yield: 24 cookies
Exchange, 1 cookie: ⅔ bread
Calories, 1 cookie: 45
Carbohydrates, 1 cookie: 8 g

Banana-Cake Cookies

8-oz. box	pound cake mix, fructose-sweetened	227-g box
⅔ c.	mashed banana*	180 mL
1	egg white	1
½ c.	dietetic frosting mix	125 mL
2 T.	skim milk	30 mL
1 T.	margarine	15 mL

*One large banana.

Combine cake mix, ⅓ c. (90 mL) of the mashed banana, and egg white in a medium-size bowl. Stir to blend completely. (Mix will seem sticky.) Drop on a cool, greased cookie sheet. Bake at 375°F (190°C) for 12 to 15 minutes or until golden brown. Move to cooling rack. Meanwhile, in a saucepan, combine the frosting mix, the remaining ⅓ c. (90 mL) mashed banana, and the skim milk. Stir to blend; then place saucepan over medium heat and continue stirring until mixture is very thick and pastelike. Remove from heat, and stir in the margarine. Cool completely before frosting cookies.

Yield: 24 cookies
Exchange, 1 cookie: ½ bread, ⅓ fat
Calories, 1 cookie: 52
Carbohydrates, 1 cookie: 8 g

Bar Cookies

Light Chocolate Bars

1 c.	all-purpose flour	250 mL
1 c.	quick-cooking oatmeal	250 mL
¼ c.	granulated fructose	60 mL
¼ t.	baking soda	1 mL
¼ c.	vegetable shortening	60 mL
1	egg white	1
⅔ c.	water	180 mL
¼ c.	dry powdered milk	60 mL
2 T.	granulated fructose	30 mL
4 t.	cornstarch	20 mL
2 oz.	baking chocolate	56 g
1 t.	vanilla extract	5 mL
¼ c.	sliced almonds	60 mL

Combine flour, oatmeal, the ¼ c. (60 mL) of fructose, baking soda, vegetable shortening, and egg white in a large mixing bowl. Cut into large coarse crumbs. Press into the bottom of an ungreased 11 × 7 in. (28 × 18 cm) pan. Set aside. Combine water, powdered milk, the 2 T. (30 mL) of granulated fructose, and cornstarch in a saucepan. Stir to completely blend. Add baking chocolate. Cook and stir over medium heat until mixture is thick and bubbly. Remove from heat; stir in vanilla. Spread over crumb layer in pan. Sprinkle with sliced almonds. Lightly press almonds into chocolate layer. Bake at 350°F (175°C) for 25 minutes or until chocolate layer is set. Allow to cool, and cut into 35 bars.

Yield: 35 bars
Exchange, 1 bar: ½ bread, ⅓ fat
Calories, 1 bar: 50
Carbohydrates, 1 bar: 6 g

Raisin Squares

1 c.	all-purpose flour	250 mL
1 c.	quick-cooking oatmeal	250 mL
⅓ c.	granulated fructose	90 mL
¼ t.	baking soda	1 mL
½ c.	margarine	125 mL
¾ c.	cold water	190 mL
1 T.	cornstarch	15 mL
1 c.	raisins	250 mL
1 t.	finely grated orange peel	5 mL

Combine flour, oatmeal, fructose, and baking soda in a large mixing bowl; stir to mix. Cut in the margarine until mixture is coarse crumbs. Remove ½ c. (125 mL) and set aside. Press remaining crumbs into an ungreased 9-in. (23-cm) shiny baking pan. Combine cold water and cornstarch in a small saucepan. Stir to blend. Add raisins and orange peel. Stir and cook over medium heat until mixture is thick and bubbly. Spread over crumb layer in baking pan. Sprinkle reserved crumbs over raisin mixture. Lightly press top crumbs into raisin layer. Bake at 350°F (175°C) for 30 minutes. Cool in pan on a cooling rack. Cut into 25 squares.

Yield: 25 squares
Exchange, 1 square: 1 bread
Calories, 1 square: 92
Carbohydrates, 1 square: 14 g

Cocoa Brownies

6 T.	low-calorie margarine	90 mL
½ c.	granulated fructose	125 mL
½ c.	cocoa powder	125 mL
1 t.	vanilla extract	5 mL
2	egg whites	2
½ c.	all-purpose flour	125 mL
1 t.	aspartame sweetener	5 mL

Melt margarine in a medium-size saucepan. Blend in fructose, and stir until creamy. Remove from heat. Stir in cocoa powder and vanilla extract until completely blended. Thoroughly stir in egg whites. Blend in flour. Pour into a lightly greased 8-in. (20-cm) shiny pan; spread mixture evenly over bottom of pan. Bake at 350°F (175°C) for 25 minutes or until dough begins to loosen on the sides of the pan. Remove from oven; sprinkle with aspartame sweetener. Cool in pan on a cooling rack. Cut into 16 brownies.

Yield: 16 brownies
Exchange, 1 brownie: ½ bread, 1 fat
Calories, 1 brownie: 86
Carbohydrates, 1 brownie: 7 g

Currant Bars

½ c.	low-calorie margarine	125 mL
¼ c.	granulated fructose	60 mL
1 t.	finely grated lemon peel	5 mL
1	egg	1
1	egg white	1
1¼ c.	all-purpose flour	310 mL
¼ t.	baking powder	1 mL
⅓ c.	currants	90 mL
¼ c.	sliced almonds	60 mL
2 t.	aspartame sweetener	10 mL

Beat margarine until light and fluffy. Scrape down bowl; then add fructose and beat for at least 1 minute. Mixture should be creamy. Beat in lemon peel and egg. Beat in egg white. Combine flour and baking powder in a bowl; stir to mix. Add to creamed mixture, and beat until completely blended. Lightly spray a 13 × 9 in. (33 × 23 cm) cookie sheet or pan with vegetable-oil spray. Transfer cookie dough to pan. Spread evenly over bottom of pan. To ease spreading, dampen a knife in a glass of hot water. Sprinkle surface of dough with currants and almonds; press them into the dough. Bake at 350°F (175°C) for 12 to 13 minutes. Remove pan from oven. Sprinkle with aspartame sweetener. Cut into 35 bars. Cool in pan on a rack. Remove bars from pan when cool.

Yield: 35 bars
Exchange, 1 bar: ⅓ bread, ½ fat
Calories, 1 bar: 56
Carbohydrates, 1 bar: 5 g

Pineapple Coconut Bars

½ c.	low-calorie margarine	125 mL
¼ c.	granulated fructose	60 mL
½ t.	grated lemon peel	2 mL
1	egg	1
1	egg white	1
1¼ c.	all-purpose flour	310 mL
¼ t.	baking powder	1 mL
¾ c.	unsweetened dried pineapple	190 mL
¼ c.	unsweetened grated coconut	60 mL

Beat margarine until light and fluffy. Scrape down bowl; then add fructose and beat for at least 1 minute. Mixture should be creamy. Beat in lemon peel and egg thoroughly. Beat in egg white. Combine flour and baking powder in a bowl; stir to mix. Add to creamed mixture, and beat until completely blended. Lightly spray a 13 × 9 in. (33 × 23 cm) cookie sheet or pan with vegetable-oil spray. Transfer cookie dough to pan. Spread evenly over bottom of pan. To ease spreading, dampen a knife in a glass of hot water. Chop dried pineapple into small pieces. Combine pineapple pieces and coconut in a small bowl. Mix to blend. Sprinkle mixture over cookie layer in pan. Firmly press mixture into the dough. Bake at 350°F (175°C) for 25 minutes, or until done. Cool in pan on cooling rack. Cut into 48 bars.

Yield: 48 bars
Exchange, 1 bar: ½ bread, ¼ fat
Calories, 1 bar: 43
Carbohydrates, 1 bar: 6 g

Moist Buttermilk Brownies

2 c.	all-purpose flour	500 mL
½ c.	granulated fructose	125 mL
1 t.	baking soda	5 mL
1 c.	water	250 mL
¾ c.	low-calorie margarine	190 mL
⅓ c.	unsweetened cocoa powder	90 mL
½ c.	buttermilk	125 mL
2	eggs	2
2 t.	vanilla extract	10 mL

Combine flour, fructose, and baking soda in a large mixing bowl. Combine water, margarine, and cocoa powder in a saucepan. Cook and stir over medium heat until mixture comes to a rolling boil. Remove from heat. Pour into flour mixture. Beat until thoroughly blended. Measure buttermilk into a 1- or 2-cup (250- or 500-mL) measuring cup. Blend eggs, one at a time, into buttermilk; stir in vanilla. Pour buttermilk mixture into chocolate dough. Beat for 1 minute or until mixture is very creamy. Pour into a 14 × 10 in. (36 × 25 cm) greased cookie sheet. Bake at 350°F (175°C) for 25 minutes or until toothpick inserted in middle comes out clean. Move to cooling rack. Cool for 10 minutes. Cut into 48 brownies. Cool completely in pan.

Yield: 48 brownies
Exchange, 1 brownie: ½ bread
Calories, 1 brownie: 52
Carbohydrates, 1 brownie: 6 g

Mixed-Fruit Squares

1 c.	all-purpose flour	250 mL
1 c.	quick-cooking oatmeal	250 mL
⅓ c.	granulated fructose	90 mL
¼ t.	baking soda	1 mL
½ c.	soft margarine	125 mL
¾ c.	cold water	190 mL
1 T.	cornstarch	15 mL
1 c.	unsweetened dried mixed fruit	250 mL

Combine flour, oatmeal, fructose, and baking soda in a large mixing bowl; stir to mix. Cut in the margarine until mixture is coarse crumbs. Remove ½ c. (125 mL) and set aside. Press remaining crumbs into an ungreased 9-in. (23-cm) shiny baking pan. Combine cold water and cornstarch in a small saucepan. Stir to blend. Add mixed dried fruit. Stir and cook over medium heat until mixture is thick and bubbly. Spread over crumb layer in pan. Sprinkle reserved crumbs over fruit mixture. Lightly press top crumbs into fruit layer. Bake at 350°F (175°C) for 30 minutes. Cool in pan on a wire rack. Cut into 25 squares.

Yield: 25 squares
Exchange, 1 square: 1 bread
Calories, 1 square: 89
Carbohydrates, 1 square: 14 g

Lemon Poppy-Seed Bars

2 c.	pancake mix	500 mL
8-oz. carton	lemon yogurt	224-g carton
2	eggs	2
¼ c.	cooking oil	60 mL
2 T.	poppy seeds	30 mL

Combine pancake mix, lemon yogurt, eggs, and cooking oil in a mixing bowl. Mix until blended. Beat for 2 more minutes. Stir in poppy seeds. Pour into a greased 13 × 9 in. (33 × 23 cm) baking pan. Bake at 350°F (175°C) for 25 to 30 minutes or until toothpick inserted in middle comes out clean. Cut into 32 bars.

Yield: 32 bars
Exchange, 1 bar: ⅓ bread, ⅓ fat
Calories, 1 bar: 42
Carbohydrates, 1 bar: 5 g

Spiced-Fruit Bars

⅓ c.	low-calorie margarine	90 mL
¼ c.	creamy peanut butter	60 mL
1¼ c.	all-purpose flour	310 mL
¼ c.	granulated fructose	60 mL
8-oz pkg.	light cream cheese, softened	227-g pkg.
1 T.	water	15 mL
2 T.	all-purpose flour	30 mL
1 t.	ground cinnamon	5 mL
½ t.	ground nutmeg	2 mL
3	egg whites	3
½ c.	unsweetened dried mixed fruit, finely chopped	125 mL

Combine margarine and peanut butter in a medium-size mixing bowl. Beat to blend. Add half of the ¼ c. (310 mL) of flour and the ¼ c. (60 mL) of fructose. Beat well (mixture will stick to the beaters of the mixer). Push mixture from beaters, and add remaining flour. Beat until mixture is fine crumbs. Transfer to a 13 × 9 in. (33 × 23 cm.) ungreased, shiny baking pan. Bake at 350°F (175°C) for 15 minutes or until surface is lightly browned. Meanwhile, combine cream cheese, water, the 2 T. (30 mL) of flour, cinnamon, and nutmeg in a mixing bowl. (The same bowl can be used.) Beat until well blended. Add the egg whites; beat until thoroughly combined. Stir in the mixed fruit. Pour over the baked dough. Return to oven, and bake for 15 more minutes or until cream-cheese mixture is set. Remove from oven to cooling rack. Cool completely. Cut into 48 bars.

Yield: 48 bars
Exchange, 1 bar: ⅓ bread, ¼ fat
Calories, 1 bar: 32
Carbohydrates, 1 bar: 5 g

Peanut Triangles

⅓ c.	low-calorie margarine	90 mL
¼ c.	creamy peanut butter	60 mL
1¼ c.	all-purpose flour	310 mL
¼ c.	granulated fructose	60 mL
8-oz. pkg.	light cream cheese, softened	227-g pkg.
1 T.	water	15 mL
2 T.	granulated fructose	30 mL
2 T.	all-purpose flour	30 mL
1	egg	1
2	egg whites	2
½ c.	finely chopped peanuts	125 mL

Combine margarine and peanut butter in a medium-size mixing bowl. Beat to blend. Add half of the 1¼ c. (310 mL) flour and the ¼ c. (60 mL) of fructose. Beat well (mixture will stick to the beaters of the mixer). Push mixture from beaters, and add remaining flour. Beat until mixture is fine crumbs. Transfer to a 13 × 9 in. (33 × 23 cm) ungreased, shiny baking pan. Bake at 350°F (175°C) for 15 minutes, or until surface is lightly browned. Meanwhile, combine cream cheese, water, the 2 T. (30 mL) of fructose, and the 2 T. (30 mL) of flour in a mixing bowl. (The same bowl can be used.) Beat until well blended. Add the egg and egg whites; beat until thoroughly combined. Stir in the chopped peanuts. Pour over the baked dough. Return to oven, and bake for 15 more minutes or until cream-cheese mixture is set. Remove from oven to cooling rack. Cool completely. Cut into 24 squares; then cut each square in half diagonally.

Yield: 48 triangles
Exchange, 1 triangle: ⅓ bread, ¼ fat
Calories, 1 triangle: 36
Carbohydrates, 1 triangle: 4 g

Lemon Cheese Bars

½ c.	low-calorie margarine	125 mL
¼ c.	granulated fructose	60 mL
1 t.	finely grated lemon peel	5 mL
2	egg whites	2
1¼ c.	all-purpose flour	310 mL
¼ t.	baking powder	1 mL
8-oz. pkg.	light cream cheese, softened	227-g pkg.
2 T.	lemon juice	30 mL
2 T.	all-purpose flour	30 mL
1 T.	freshly grated lemon rind	15 mL
1 t.	lemon flavoring or oil	5 mL
3	egg whites	3

Beat margarine until light and fluffy. Scrape down bowl; then add fructose and beat for at least 1 minute. Mixture should be creamy. Beat in lemon peel. Beat in egg whites. Combine flour and baking powder in a bowl; stir to mix. Add to creamed mixture, and beat until completely blended. Lightly spray a 13 × 9 in. (33 × 23 cm) cookie sheet or pan with vegetable-oil spray. Transfer cookie dough to pan. Spread evenly over bottom of pan. To ease spreading, dampen a knife in a glass of hot water. Bake at 350°F (175°C) for 12 to 13 minutes. Remove pan from oven. Meanwhile, combine cream cheese, lemon juice, flour, lemon rind, and flavoring in a mixing bowl. Beat until well blended. Add the egg whites; beat until thoroughly combined. Pour over the baked dough. Return to oven, and bake for 15 more minutes or until cream-cheese mixture is set. Remove from oven to cooling rack. Cool completely. Cut into 48 bars.

Yield: 48 bars
Exchange, 1 bar: ⅓ bread
Calories, 1 bar: 28
Carbohydrates, 1 bar: 4 g

Plain & Simple Cake Brownies

1 T.	margarine, melted	15 mL
1 oz.	unsweetened baking chocolate, melted	28 g
1 c.	all-purpose flour	250 mL
½ t.	cream of tartar	2 mL
¼ t.	baking soda	1 mL

| 1 | egg | 1 | |
| 2 T. | buttermilk | 30 mL | |

Combine melted margarine and baking chocolate in a bowl. Stir to blend. Combine flour, cream of tartar, and baking soda in another bowl. Stir to mix. Slightly beat egg and buttermilk together in a small bowl or cup. Stir egg mixture into chocolate mixture. Gradually beat flour mixture into chocolate mixture until creamy. Spread into the bottom of a 7 × 11 in. (17 × 27 cm) greased and floured cake pan. Dough will spread easier if you use a dampened spreading knife. Bake at 350°F (175°C) for 10 minutes, or until brownies are firm on top. Cool slightly in pan. Turn out onto cutting board; cut into 28 brownies.

Yield: 28 brownies
Exchange, 1 brownie: ⅓ bread
Calories, 1 brownie: 26
Carbohydrates, 1 brownie: 3 g

Soft Rice Bars

¼ c.	cold water	60 mL
1 env.	unflavored gelatin	1 env.
1 T.	granulated fructose	15 mL
1 T.	granulated sugar replacement	15 mL
2 T.	margarine	30 mL
1	egg white	1
6 c.	crisp rice cereal	1500 mL

In a microwaveable bowl or saucepan, sprinkle the gelatin over the cold water; then allow the gelatin to soften for 5 minutes. Heat until gelatin is completely dissolved. Remove from heat. Add fructose, sugar replacement, and margarine. Stir to dissolve fructose and melt margarine. Allow mixture to cool to a thick syrup. Beat egg white to soft peaks. Continue beating the egg white, and pour the gelatin mixture in a thin stream into it. (Mixture will not fluff up.) Place rice cereal in a large bowl. Thoroughly fold egg white–gelatin mixture into cereal. Transfer to a lightly greased 13 × 9 in. (33 × 23 cm) cake pan. Cool. Cut into 24 bars.

Yield: 24 bars
Exchange, 1 bar: ¼ bread
Calories, 1 bar: 21
Carbohydrates, 1 bar: 3 g

Rice Bars with Chocolate Chips

¼ c.	cold water	60 mL
1 env.	unflavored gelatin	1 env.
1 T.	granulated fructose	15 mL
1 T.	granulated sugar replacement	15 mL
2 T.	margarine	30 mL
1	egg white	1
6 c.	crisp rice cereal	1500 mL
½ c.	mini chocolate chips	125 mL

In a microwavable bowl or saucepan, sprinkle the gelatin over the cold water; then allow the gelatin to soften for 5 minutes. Heat until gelatin is completely dissolved. Remove from heat. Add fructose, sugar replacement, and margarine. Stir to dissolve fructose and melt margarine. Allow mixture to cool to a thick syrup. Beat egg white to soft peaks. Continue beating the egg white, and pour the gelatin mixture in a thin stream into it. (Mixture will not fluff up.) Place rice cereal in a large bowl. Thoroughly fold egg white–gelatin mixture into cereal. Fold in chocolate chips. Transfer to a lightly greased 13 × 9 in. (33 × 23 cm) cake pan. Cool. Cut into 24 bars.

Yield: 24 bars
Exchange, 1 bar: ⅓ bread
Calories, 1 bar: 23
Carbohydrates, 1 bar: 4 g

Walnut Rice Bars

¼ c.	cold water	60 mL
1 env.	unflavored gelatin	1 env.
1 T.	granulated fructose	15 mL
1 T.	granulated sugar replacement	15 mL
2 T.	margarine	30 mL
1	egg white	1
6 c.	crisp rice cereal	1500 mL
½ c.	coarsely chopped walnuts	125 mL

In a microwavable bowl or saucepan, sprinkle the gelatin over the cold water; then allow the gelatin to soften for 5 minutes. Heat until gelatin is completely dissolved. Remove from heat. Add fructose, sugar replacement, and margarine. Stir to dissolve fructose and melt margarine. Allow mixture to cool to a thick syrup. Beat egg white to soft peaks. Continue beating the egg white, and pour the gelatin mixture in a thin stream into it. (Mixture will not fluff up.) Place rice cereal in a large bowl. Thoroughly fold egg white–gelatin mixture into cereal. Fold in walnuts. Transfer to a lightly greased 13 × 9 in. (33 × 23 cm) cake pan. Cool. Cut into 24 bars.

Yield: 24 bars
Exchange, 1 bar: ⅓ bread, ¼ fat
Calories, 1 bar: 29
Carbohydrates, 1 bar: 3 g

Cherry Rice Bars

1 env.	sugar-free cherry gelatin	1 env.
(4 servings)		(4 servings)
¼ c.	hot water	60 mL
2 T.	margarine	30 mL
1	egg white	1
6 c.	crisp rice cereal	1500 mL
½ c.	dried cherries*	125 mL

*Dried cherries can be bought at many health-food stores.

Dissolve the cherry gelatin in the hot water. (If needed, heat mixture until gelatin is completely dissolved.) Stir margarine into hot gelatin until melted. Allow mixture to cool to a thick syrup. Beat egg white to soft peaks. Continue beating the egg white, and pour the gelatin mixture in a thin stream into it. (Mixture will not fluff up.) Place rice cereal in a large bowl. Thoroughly fold egg white–gelatin mixture into cereal. Pit cherries and chop into small pieces. Fold chopped cherries into mixture. Transfer to a lightly greased 13 × 9 in. (33 × 23 cm) cake pan. Cool. Cut into 24 bars.

Yield: 24 bars
Exchange, 1 bar: ⅓ bread
Calories, 1 bar: 24
Carbohydrates, 1 bar: 3 g

Whole-Wheat Pumpkin-&-Applesauce Bars with Toasted Almonds

½ c.	slivered almonds	125 mL
1 c.	pumpkin purée	250 mL
½ c.	sugar-free applesauce	125 mL
1	egg	1
2 T.	frozen apple-juice concentrate	30 mL
2 T.	granulated sugar replacement	30 mL
2 T.	granulated fructose	30 mL
2 t.	almond flavoring	10 mL
1 c.	instant whole-wheat baking mix	250 mL

Place almonds in a nonstick skillet. Place skillet over medium heat, and shake or stir almonds until lightly toasted. Pour almonds onto a cutting board and chop until coarse. Set aside. Combine pumpkin purée, applesauce, egg, apple-juice concentrate, sugar replacement, fructose, and almond flavoring in a mixing bowl. Beat to blend thoroughly. Beat in the whole-wheat baking mix until well blended. Stir in ¼ c. (60 mL) of the toasted almonds. Spray a 7 X 11 in. (17 X 27 cm) shiny cake pan with vegetable-oil spray. Pour in cookie batter, spreading evenly. Sprinkle remaining toasted almonds over top of batter. Bake at 350°F (175°C) for 40 to 45 minutes, or until toothpick inserted in middle comes out clean. Move pan to cooling rack. If desired, dust with aspartame sweetener while hot. When cool, cut into 24 bars.

Yield: 24 bars
Exchange, 1 bar: ⅓ bread, ⅓ fruit, ⅓ fat
Calories, 1 bar: 51
Carbohydrates, 1 bar: 8 g

Oat-Bran Orange Bars

Filling:

1 c.	orange juice	250 mL
2 T.	white grape-juice concentrate	30 mL
2 t.	cornstarch	10 mL
2 T.	orange peel	30 mL

Base:

1½ c.	oat-bran flour	375 mL
1 t.	baking soda	5 mL

dash	salt	dash
3 T.	liquid vegetable shortening	45 mL
2 T.	granulated fructose	30 mL
2 T.	granulated sugar replacement	30 mL
1	egg white	1

Filling: Combine orange juice, grape-juice concentrate, and cornstarch in a saucepan. Stir to dissolve cornstarch. Place over medium heat, and allow to come to a complete boil. Stir until mixture is clear and thick. Remove from heat. When mixture has cooled, stir in orange peel.

Base: Combine oat-bran flour, baking soda, salt, liquid shortening, fructose, sugar replacement, and egg white in a mixing bowl. Beat to blend thoroughly. Lightly grease a 9 × 9 in. (23 × 23 cm) shiny baking pan with vegetable-oil spray. Spread about three-fourths of the base mixture into the bottom of the pan. Spread orange filling on base-mixture surface. Add 1 T. (15 mL) of water to remaining base mixture. Drizzle over the top of orange mixture. Bake at 350°F (175°C) for about 35 to 40 minutes, or until mixture is firm. Cool on cooling rack. Cut into 36 bars.

Yield: 36 bars
Exchange, 1 bar: ⅓ bread
Calories, 1 bar: 25
Carbohydrates, 1 bar: 5 g

Cherry Brownie Bars

8.5-oz. pkg.	brownie mix, fructose-sweetened	241-g pkg.
¼ c.	all-fruit cherry preserves, melted	60 mL
2 T.	water	30 mL
1	egg	1
½ c.	unsweetened dark sweet cherries	125 mL

Combine brownie mix, melted cherry preserves, water, and egg in a bowl. Blend by hand until smooth. Cut cherries into quarters (four pieces). Stir into batter. Spread batter into a greased 8-in. (20-cm) square baking pan. Bake at 350°F (175°C) for 25 to 30 minutes, or until toothpick inserted in middle comes out clean. Cool. Cut into 16 bars.

Yield: 16 bars
Exchange, 1 bar: ½ bread, ½ fat
Calories, 1 bar: 52
Carbohydrates, 1 bar: 8 g

Brownies with Matzo Meal

3 oz.	unsweetened baking chocolate	85 g
½ c.	margarine	125 mL
1⅓ c.	granulated sugar replacement	340 mL
⅔ c.	granulated fructose	180 mL
4	eggs	4
1 c.	matzo meal	250 mL
1 T.	brandy extract	15 mL
dash	salt	dash

Melt chocolate and margarine in a saucepan over low heat. Combine chocolate mixture, sugar replacement, and fructose in a mixing bowl. Beat to blend. Add eggs, one at a time, beating well after each addition. Stir in matzo meal, brandy extract, and salt. Pour into a greased 9-in. (23-cm) square baking pan. Bake at 350°F (175°C) for 30 minutes. Cool. Cut into 36 brownies.

Yield: 36 brownies
Exchange, 1 brownie: ½ bread, ¾ fat
Calories, 1 brownie: 65
Carbohydrates, 1 brownie: 7 g

Mom's Apricot Squares

1½ c.	all-purpose flour	375 mL
1½ c.	quick-cooking oatmeal	375 mL
⅔ c.	granulated brown-sugar replacement	180 mL
⅓ c.	granulated fructose	90 mL
¾ c.	margarine	190 mL
½ c.	all-fruit apricot preserves	125 mL

Combine flour, oatmeal, brown-sugar replacement, and fructose in a bowl. Stir to mix. Add margarine. Use a pastry blender, a fork, or your fingers to crumb the mixture. Press two-thirds of the mixture into the bottom of a greased 8-in. (20-cm) baking pan. Spread with apricot preserves. Sprinkle remaining crumbs on top, pressing them down lightly. Bake at 350°F (175°C) for 30 to 35 minutes. Allow to cool in pan. Cut into 16 squares.

Yield: 16 squares
Exchange, 1 bar: ½ bread, ½ fat
Calories, 1 bar: 60
Carbohydrates, 1 bar: 8 g

Cottage-Cheese Bars

Filling:

1 c.	low-fat cottage cheese	250 mL
¼ c.	low-fat milk	60 mL
1 T.	cornstarch	15 mL
1 T.	granulated fructose	15 mL
1 T.	granulated sugar replacement	15 mL
1 T.	cinnamon	15 mL
½ t.	ground nutmeg	2 mL
¼ t.	ground cloves	1 mL
¼ t.	ground ginger	1 mL

Base:

⅓ c.	margarine	90 mL
2 T.	granulated fructose	30 mL
2 T.	granulated sugar replacement	30 mL
1	egg white	1
1 c.	all-purpose flour	250 mL
1 t.	baking powder	5 mL
2 c.	quick-cooking oatmeal	500 mL

Filling: Combine cottage cheese, milk, cornstarch, fructose, sugar replacement, and spices in a saucepan. Stir to completely dissolve cornstarch. Place saucepan over medium heat, and stir until mixture comes to a full rolling boil. Remove from heat. Stir occasionally until mixture has cooled.

Base: Cream margarine, fructose, and sugar replacement. Beat in egg white. Add flour and baking powder. Beat well. Blend in 1¾ c. (440 mL) of the oatmeal. Press three-fourths of the base mixture into the bottom of a 9 × 9 in. (23 × 23 cm) shiny baking pan. Spread with cooled cottage-cheese filling. Add remaining ¼ c. (60 mL) of the oatmeal to the remaining base mixture. Crumb with a fork or with your hands. Sprinkle crumb mixture over cookie surface. Bake at 350°F (175°C) for 25 to 30 minutes. Cool on cooling rack. Cut into 36 bars.

Yield: 36 bars
Exchange, 1 bar: ½ bread, ¼ fat
Calories, 1 bar: 56
Carbohydrates, 1 bar: 7 g

Coconut Pecan Bars

Base:

¼ c.	margarine	60 mL
1 c.	all-purpose flour	250 mL

Filling:

2	eggs	2
1 T.	granulated fructose	15 mL
3 T.	granulated sugar replacement	45 mL
1 t.	vanilla extract	5 mL
½ c.	unsweetened coconut*	125 mL
¼ c.	finely ground pecans	60 mL
⅛ t.	baking powder	½ mL

*Unsweetened coconut can be bought at most health-food stores.

Base: Cut margarine into flour in a bowl until mixture crumbles. Press crumb mixture into an ungreased 7 × 11 in. (17 × 27 cm) baking pan. Bake at 350°F (175°C) for 12 to 15 minutes, or until lightly browned.

Filling: Beat eggs in a bowl until light and lemon-colored. Gradually beat in fructose, sugar replacement, and vanilla extract Stir in coconut, pecans, and baking powder. Spread mixture over baked base. Return to oven, and continue baking for 20 minutes more, or until surface is lightly tanned. Cool on rack. Cut into 45 bars.

Yield: 45 bars
Exchange, 1 bar: ¼ bread, ⅓ fat
Calories, 1 bar: 39
Carbohydrates, 1 bar: 2 g

Date Custard Bars

Base:

¼ c.	margarine	60 mL
1 c.	all-purpose flour	250 mL

Filling:

2	eggs	2
1 T.	granulated fructose	15 mL
3 T.	granulated sugar replacement	45 mL
1 t.	vanilla extract	5 mL
½ c.	finely chopped dates	125 mL

| 1 T. | all-purpose flour | 15 mL |
| 1/8 t. | baking powder | 1/2 mL |

Base: Cut margarine into flour in a bowl until mixture crumbles. Press crumb mixture into an ungreased 7 × 11 in. (17 × 27 cm) baking pan. Bake at 350°F (175°C) for 12 to 15 minutes, or until lightly browned.

Filling: Beat eggs in a bowl until light and lemon-colored. Gradually beat in fructose, sugar replacement, and vanilla extract. Combine dates and flour in a bowl; then flip or stir to cover all date pieces lightly with the flour. Stir dates and baking powder into custard mixture. Spread mixture over baked base. Return to oven, and continue baking for 20 minutes more, or until surface is lightly tanned. Cool on rack. Cut into 45 bars.

Yield: 45 bars
Exchange, 1 bar: 1/3 bread, 1/3 fat
Calories, 1 bar: 41
Carbohydrates, 1 bar: 3 g

Butterscotch Bars

1 c.	all-purpose flour	250 mL
1 t.	baking powder	5 mL
dash	salt	dash
1/4 c.	melted margarine	60 mL
1/2 c.	granulated brown-sugar replacement	125 mL
1	egg	1
1 t.	vanilla extract	5 mL
1 t.	liquid butter flavoring	5 mL

Sift together flour, baking powder, and salt. Set aside. Combine margarine and brown-sugar replacement in a bowl. Beat or stir to blend. Add egg, vanilla extract, and liquid butter flavoring. Mix well. Gradually stir flour mixture into margarine mixture. Lightly grease an 8 × 8 in. (20 × 20 cm) baking pan with vegetable-oil spray. Spread mixture into bottom of pan. Bake at 350°F (175°C) for 30 minutes, or until top springs back when touched. Cool in pan on cooling rack. Cut into 36 bars.

Yield: 36 bars
Exchange, 1 bar: 1/4 bread
Calories, 1 bar: 22
Carbohydrates, 1 bar: 2 g

Raspberry Bars

Base:

1 c.	all-purpose flour	250 mL
¼ c.	margarine	60 mL

Filling:

10-oz. jar	all-fruit spreadable raspberry jam	283-g jar

Base: Cut margarine into flour in a bowl until mixture crumbles. Press crumb mixture into an ungreased 7 × 11 in. (17 × 27 cm) baking pan.

Filling: Spoon jam into a microwavable mixing bowl. Either heat the jam to a liquid or stir until jam is very soft. Lightly spread jam over surface of base. You won't have to cover the full base. Bake at 350°F (175°C) for 30 minutes. After 15 to 20 minutes, turn and twist pan to allow the hot jam to cover the full surface of the base. Cool on rack. Cut into 40 bars.

Yield: 41 bars
Exchange, 1 bar: ½ fruit, ¼ fat
Calories, 1 bar: 32
Carbohydrates, 1 bar: 6 g

Pineapple Coconut Bars

½ c.	margarine	125 mL
⅔ c.	granulated sugar replacement	180 mL
⅓ c.	granulated fructose	90 mL
2	eggs	2
½ t.	almond flavoring	2 mL
¾ c.	all-purpose flour	190 mL
1 t.	baking powder	5 mL
8-oz. can	crushed pineapple in juice	227-g can
½ c.	unsweetened flaked coconut*	125 mL

*Unsweetened flaked coconut can be bought at health-food stores.

Combine margarine, sugar replacement, and fructose in a large mixing bowl. Beat until mixture is well blended and creamy. Add eggs and almond flavoring. Beat well. Combine flour and baking powder. Gradually beat flour mixture into margarine mixture. Drain pineapple thoroughly. Stir coconut and drained pineapple into batter. Spread mixture evenly over the bottom of a greased 9-in. (23-cm) square baking pan. Bake at 350°F (175°C) for 25 to 30 minutes. Allow to cool in pan. Cut into 36 bars.

Yield: 36 bars
Exchange, 1 bar: ⅓ bread, ⅓ fat
Calories, 1 bar: 50
Carbohydrates, 1 bar: 4 g

Oatmeal Applesauce Bars

Filling:

2 T.	margarine	30 mL
¾ c.	unsweetened applesauce	190 mL
1 t.	vanilla extract	5 mL
1 t.	apple-pie spices	5 mL
2 t.	cornstarch	10 mL

Base:

½ c.	margarine	125 mL
¼ c.	fructose	60 mL
2 T.	granulated sugar replacement	30 mL
1	egg	1
1 t.	vanilla extract	5 mL
1 t.	apple-pie spices	5 mL
¾ c.	all-purpose flour	190 mL
½ t.	baking soda	2 mL
2 c.	quick-cooking oatmeal	500 mL

Filling: Combine margarine, applesauce, vanilla extract, apple-pie spices, and cornstarch in a saucepan. Stir to completely dissolve cornstarch. Place saucepan over medium heat, and stir until mixture comes to a full rolling boil. Remove from heat. Stir occasionally until mixture has cooled.

Base: Cream margarine, fructose, and sugar replacement. Beat in egg, vanilla extract, and apple-pie spices. Add flour and baking soda. Beat well. Blend in 1¾ c. (440 mL) of the oatmeal. Press three-fourths of the base mixture into the bottom of a 9 × 9 in. (23 × 23 cm) shiny baking pan. Spread with cooled applesauce filling. Add remaining ¼ c. (60 mL) of the oatmeal to the remaining base mixture. Crumb with a fork or with your hands. Sprinkle crumb mixture over cookie surface. Bake at 350°F (175°C) for 25 to 30 minutes. Cool on cooling rack. Cut into 36 bars.

Yield: 36 bars
Exchange, 1 bar: ½ bread, ¾ fat
Calories, 1 bar: 73
Carbohydrates, 1 bar: 9 g

Oatmeal Chocolate Bars

Filling:

2 T.	margarine	30 mL
½ c.	semisweet chocolate chips	125 mL
¾ c.	evaporated milk	190 mL
1 T.	chocolate flavoring	15 mL
2 t.	cornstarch	10 mL

Base:

½ c.	margarine	125 mL
¼ c.	fructose	60 mL
2 T.	granulated sugar replacement	30 mL
1	egg	1
1 t.	vanilla extract	5 mL
1 c.	all-purpose flour	250 mL
½ t.	baking soda	2 mL
2 c.	quick-cooking oatmeal	500 mL

Filling: Combine margarine, chocolate chips, evaporated milk, chocolate flavoring, and cornstarch in saucepan. Stir to completely dissolve cornstarch. Place saucepan over medium heat, and stir until mixture comes to a full rolling boil. Remove from heat. Stir occasionally until mixture has cooled.

Base: Cream margarine, fructose, and sugar replacement. Beat in egg and vanilla extract. Add flour and baking soda. Beat well. Blend in 1¾ c. (440 mL) of the oatmeal. Press three-fourths of the base mixture into the bottom of a 9 × 9 in. (23 × 23 cm) shiny baking pan. Spread with cooled chocolate filling. Add remaining ¼ c. (60 mL) of the oatmeal to the remaining base mixture. Crumb with a fork or your hands. Sprinkle crumb mixture over cookie surface. Bake at 350°F (175°C) for 25 to 30 minutes. Cool on cooling rack. Cut into 36 bars.

Yield: 36 bars
Exchange, 1 bar: ½ bread, ¾ fat
Calories, 1 bar: 72
Carbohydrates, 1 bar: 8 g

Butterscotch Brownies

1 c.	all-purpose flour	250 mL
1 t.	baking powder	5 mL

dash	salt	dash
¼ c.	melted margarine	60 mL
½ c.	granulated brown-sugar replacement	125 mL
1	egg	1
1 t.	vanilla extract	5 mL
1 t.	liquid butter flavoring	5 mL
2 oz.	semisweet baking chocolate	58 g
2 T.	margarine	30 mL

Sift together flour, baking powder, and salt. Set aside. Combine the ¼ c. (60 mL) of melted margarine and brown-sugar replacement in a bowl. Beat or stir to blend. Add egg, vanilla extract, and liquid butter flavoring. Mix well. Gradually stir flour mixture into margarine mixture. Lightly grease an 8 × 8 in. (20 × 20 cm) baking pan with vegetable-oil spray. Spread mixture into bottom of pan. Bake at 350°F (175°C) for 30 minutes, or until top springs backed when touched. Cool in pan on cooling rack. Melt semisweet baking chocolate and the 2 T. (30 mL) of margarine in a small saucepan over low heat. Cool slightly; then pour and spread over top. Allow to cool. Cut into 36 brownies.

Yield: 36 brownies
Exchange, 1 brownie: ¼ bread, ¼ fat
Calories, 1 brownie: 29
Carbohydrates, 1 brownie: 2 g

Date Brownie Bars

¾ c.	pitted dates	190 mL
8.5-oz. pkg.	brownie mix, fructose-sweetened	241-g pkg.
⅓ c.	water	90 mL
1	egg	1

Cut dates into bite-size pieces. Combine dates and brownie mix in a bowl. Stir or flip to cover, and separate date pieces. Add water and egg; blend by hand until smooth. Spread batter into a greased 8-in. (20-cm) square baking pan. Bake at 350°F (175°C) for 25 to 30 minutes, or until toothpick inserted in middle comes out clean. Cool. Cut into 16 bars.

Yield: 16 bars
Exchange, 1 bar: ¾ bread, ½ fat
Calories, 1 bar: 69
Carbohydrates, 1 bar: 12 g

Lemon Coconut Bars

Base:

¼ c.	margarine	60 mL
1 c.	all-purpose flour	250 mL

Filling:

2	eggs	2
1 T.	granulated fructose	15 mL
3 T.	granulated sugar replacement	45 mL
1 t.	vanilla extract	5 mL
¾ c.	unsweetened coconut*	190 mL
⅛ t.	baking powder	½ mL

Lemon Icing:

¼ c.	granulated fructose	60 mL
3 T.	granulated sugar replacement	45 mL
1 T.	cornstarch	15 mL
2 t.	aspartame sweetener	5 mL
1 t.	grated lemon rind	5 mL
	lemon juice	

*Unsweetened coconut can be bought at most health-food stores.

Base: Cut margarine into flour in a bowl until mixture crumbles. Press crumb mixture into an ungreased 7 × 11 in. (17 × 27 cm) baking pan. Bake at 350°F (175°C) for 12 to 15 minutes, or until lightly browned.

Filling: Beat eggs in a bowl until light and lemon-colored. Gradually beat in fructose, sugar replacement, and vanilla extract. Stir in coconut and baking powder. Spread mixture over baked base. Return to oven, and continue baking for 20 minutes more, or until surface is lightly tanned. Cool on rack.

Icing: Combine fructose, sugar replacement, cornstarch, and aspartame sweetener in a small food-blender container. Blend, turning the blender from HIGH to OFF for about 10 seconds. Pour mixture into a small mixing bowl. Add lemon rind. Stir in just enough lemon juice to make mixture smooth and of a thick liquid consistency. Drizzle over cooled base and filling; then cut into 45 bars.

Yield: 45 bars
Exchange, 1 bar: ¼ bread, ¼ fat
Calories, 1 bar: 29
Carbohydrates, 1 bar: 2 g

Easy Brownies

¼ c.	margarine	60 mL
3 oz.	unsweetened baking chocolate	85 g
1 c.	granulated sugar replacement	250 mL
¼ c.	granulated fructose	60 mL
2	eggs	2
½ c.	self-rising flour	125 mL
1 t.	vanilla extract	5 mL

Combine margarine and baking chocolate in a small saucepan. Cook over medium heat until melted. Remove from heat. Pour chocolate mixture into a mixing bowl. Add sugar replacement, fructose, and eggs. Beat until well blended. Stir in flour and vanilla. Grease a 9 × 9 in (23 × 23 cm) shiny baking pan. Spread mixture in baking pan. Bake at 350°F (175°C) for 30 minutes, or until a slight imprint remains in surface when lightly touched. Cool completely in pan. Cut into 36 brownies.

Yield: 36 brownies
Exchange, 1 brownie: ¼ bread, ½ fat
Calories, 1 brownie: 39
Carbohydrates, 1 brownie: 2 g

Cherry Vanilla Bars

8-oz. pkg.	pound cake mix, fructose-sweetened	227-g pkg.
3 T.	low-fat cherry vanilla yogurt	45 mL
1 t.	cherry flavoring	5 mL
1	egg white	1
2 T.	chopped dried cherries*	30 mL

*Chopped dried cherries can be bought at health-food stores.

Combine cake mix, yogurt, cherry flavoring, and egg white in a bowl. Stir to mix thoroughly. Fold in dried cherries. Spread evenly in the bottom of a 9 × 9 in. (23 × 23 cm) baking pan. Bake at 350°F (175°C) for 20 to 25 minutes. Allow to cool in pan. Cut into 36 bars.

Yield: 36 bars
Exchange, 1 bar: ⅓ bread
Calories, 1 bar: 27
Carbohydrates, 1 bar: 4 g

Cinnamon Brownies

2 c.	all-purpose flour	500 mL
½ c.	granulated sugar replacement	125 mL
¼ c.	granulated fructose	60 mL
1 t.	baking soda	5 mL
dash	salt	dash
¾ t.	ground cinnamon	4 mL
1 c.	margarine	250 mL
1 c.	water	250 mL
3 T.	baking cocoa	45 mL
½ c.	buttermilk	125 mL
2	eggs	2
2 t.	vanilla extract	10 mL

Sift together flour, sugar replacement, fructose, baking soda, salt, and cinnamon. Combine margarine, water, and baking cocoa in a saucepan. Cook over low heat until margarine is melted. Beat cocoa mixture into dry flour mixture. Add buttermilk, eggs, and vanilla extract. Beat for 2 minutes. Grease a 15 × 10 in. (39 × 25 cm) jelly-roll pan. Pour brownie mixture into pan, spreading evenly. Bake at 350°F (175°C) for 25 minutes, or until top springs back when lightly touched. Cool slightly in pan before cutting into 50 brownies.

Yield: 50 brownies
Exchange, 1 brownie: ⅓ bread
Calories, 1 brownie: 37
Carbohydrates, 1 brownie: 4 g

Pear Bars

16-oz. can	pears in juice	454-g can
2 c.	all-purpose flour	500 mL
⅔ c.	granulated sugar replacement	190 mL
⅓ c.	granulated fructose	90 mL
2 t.	baking soda	10 mL
2	eggs	2
¼ c.	margarine, softened	60 mL

Drain juice from pears into a large mixing bowl; reserve juice. Cut pears into chunks, and place into bowl with juice. Add flour, sugar replacement, fructose, baking soda, eggs, and margarine. Beat well, at least 2 minutes. Pour batter into a greased 13 × 9 in. (33 × 23 cm) baking pan. Bake at

350°F (175°C) for 30 to 35 minutes or until toothpick inserted in middle comes out clean. Cool. Cut into 32 bars.

Yield: 32 bars
Exchange, 1 bar: ½ bread, ¼ fat
Calories, 1 bar: 45
Carbohydrates, 1 bar: 7 g

Pineapple Oatmeal Bars

Base:

1 c.	quick-cooking oatmeal	250 mL
½ c.	all-purpose flour	125 mL
2 T.	granulated fructose	30 mL
¼ t.	baking soda	1 mL
dash	salt	dash
⅓ c.	margarine	90 mL

Filling:

8-oz. can	crushed pineapple in juice	227-g can
1 T.	cornstarch	15 mL
3 T.	granulated sugar replacement	45 mL
¼ c.	low-fat milk	60 mL
1	egg yolk	1
1 t.	pineapple flavoring	5 mL

Base: Combine oatmeal flour, fructose, baking soda, and salt in a mixing bowl. Cut and work margarine into dry mixture until mixture is in small crumbs. Lightly grease a 11 × 7 in. (17 × 27 cm) baking pan with vegetable-oil spray. Press three-fourths of the mixture into the bottom of the pan. Reserve remaining base for topping.

Filling: Combine pineapple with juice, cornstarch, sugar replacement, milk, and egg yolk in a saucepan. Cook over medium heat, stirring constantly, until mixture is thick. Remove from heat. Stir in pineapple flavoring. Pour filling over base. Sprinkle with reserved base. Bake at 375°F (190°C) for 30 minutes, or until topping is set. Cool in pan on rack. Cut into 40 bars.

Yield: 40 bars
Exchange, 1 bar: ⅓ bread
Calories, 1 bar: 22
Carbohydrates, 1 bar: 3 g

Nut & Fruit Bars

1¾ c.	all-purpose flour	440 mL
¼ t.	baking soda	1 mL
dash	salt	dash
½ c.	margarine	125 mL
⅔ c.	granulated brown-sugar replacement	180 mL
⅓ c.	granulated fructose	90 mL
1	egg, separated	1
1 t.	vanilla extract	5 mL
1 t.	ground cinnamon	5 mL
1 t.	ground nutmeg	5 mL
¼ t.	ground cloves	1 mL
1 c.	unsweetened dried mixed fruit*	250 mL

*Unsweetened dried fruit can be bought at most health-food stores.

Sift together flour, baking soda, and salt; set aside. Using an electric mixer, beat together margarine, brown-sugar replacement, and fructose until blended thoroughly. Add egg yolk and vanilla. Beat well. Gradually stir flour mixture into creamed mixture. Mix well. (Dough will be crumbly.) Press dough into the bottom of an ungreased 13 × 9 in. (33 × 23 cm) baking pan. Beat egg white with a fork. Add cinnamon, nutmeg, cloves, and mixed fruit. Spread evenly over cookie dough in pan. Bake at 350°F (175°C) for 20 to 25 minutes. Allow to cool in pan. Cut into 54 bars.

Yield: 54 bars
Exchange, 1 bar: ⅓ bread, ⅓ fat
Calories, 1 bar: 33
Carbohydrates, 1 bar: 4 g

Great Banana Bars

Base:

1 c.	all-purpose flour	250 mL
¼ c.	margarine	60 mL

Filling:

2	very ripe bananas	2
2	eggs	2
1 t.	vanilla extract	5 mL
1 T.	all-purpose flour	15 mL
Optional:	banana flavoring	

Base: Cut margarine into flour until mixture crumbles. Press crumb mixture into an ungreased 7 × 11 in. (17 × 27 cm) baking pan.

Filling: Place bananas in a medium-size mixing bowl. Using an electric mixer, mash bananas until creamy. Add eggs and beat thoroughly. Beat in vanilla extract and flour. If desired, add banana flavoring. Pour mixture over base. Bake at 350°F (175°C) for 25 minutes. Cool on rack. Cut into 40 bars.

Yield: 40 bars
Exchange, 1 bar: ⅓ fruit, ¼ fat
Calories, 1 bar: 25
Carbohydrates, 1 bar: 4 g

Applesauce Raisin Bars

⅓ c.	margarine	90 mL
⅔ c.	granulated brown-sugar replacement	180 mL
⅓ c.	granulated fructose	90 mL
½ c.	unsweetened applesauce	125 mL
1	egg	1
1 t.	vanilla extract	5 mL
1¼ c.	all-purpose flour	310 mL
1 t.	baking powder	5 mL
½ t.	ground cinnamon	2 mL
¼ t.	baking soda	1 mL
¼ t.	ground nutmeg	1 mL
½ c.	raisins	125 mL

Melt margarine over low heat in a medium-size saucepan. Stir in brown-sugar replacement and fructose. Then stir in applesauce, egg, and vanilla. In a bowl, combine flour, baking powder, cinnamon, baking soda, and nutmeg. Stir to blend. Stir in applesauce mixture, and blend thoroughly. Stir in raisins. Spread batter evenly over the bottom of a greased 13 × 9 in. (33 × 23 cm) baking pan. Bake at 350°F (175°C) for 25 to 27 minutes, or until toothpick inserted in middle comes out clean. Allow to cool in pan. Cut into 54 bars.

Yield: 54 bars
Exchange, 1 bar: ¼ bread
Calories, 1 bar: 28
Carbohydrates, 1 bar: 3 g

Banana Walnut Bars

⅓ c.	margarine	90 mL
⅔ c.	granulated brown-sugar replacement	180 mL
⅓ c.	granulated fructose	90 mL
1	egg	1
1 t.	vanilla extract	5 mL
1 large	banana, mashed	1 large
1¾ c.	all-purpose flour	440 mL
1½ t.	baking powder	7 mL
½ c.	chopped walnuts	125 mL

Using an electric mixer, beat margarine, brown-sugar replacement, and fructose until well blended. Beat in egg, vanilla, and mashed banana. Combine flour and baking powder in another bowl. Stir to mix. Beat into banana mixture, blending thoroughly. Stir in walnuts. Spread batter evenly over the bottom of a 9-in. (23-cm) baking pan. Bake at 350°F (175°C) for 35 to 40 minutes. Allow to cool in pan. Cut into 36 bars.

Yield: 36 bars
Exchange, 1 bar: ⅓ bread, ⅓ fat
Calories, 1 bar: 46
Carbohydrates, 1 bar: 5 g

Lemon Bars

2 c.	all-purpose flour	500 mL
⅔ c.	granulated sugar replacement	180 mL
⅓ c.	granulated fructose	90 mL
1 t.	baking powder	5 mL
1 t.	freshly grated lemon peel	5 mL
9 T.	firm margarine	135 mL
2	egg yolks	2

Combine flour, sugar replacement, fructose, baking powder, and lemon peel in a large mixing bowl. Add margarine and rub with your fingers until mixture resembles cornmeal. Add egg yolks, and blend thoroughly. Press mixture into the bottom of a greased 9-in. (23-cm) baking pan. Bake at 350°F (175°C) for 15 to 20 minutes, or until top is lightly tanned. Allow to cool in pan. Cut into 36 bars.

Yield: 36 bars
Exchange, 1 bar: ½ bread
Calories, 1 bar: 37
Carbohydrates, 1 bar: 6 g

Mixed-Fruit Bars

Base:

1¾ c.	all-purpose flour	440 mL
¼ t.	baking soda	1 mL
dash	salt	dash
½ c.	margarine	125 mL
¼ c.	granulated sugar replacement	60 mL
3 T.	granulated fructose	45 mL
1	egg yolk	1

Filling:

¾ c.	unsweetened mixed dried fruit*	190 mL
1	egg white	1
1 t.	vanilla extract	5 mL
1 T.	granulated sugar replacement	15 mL
1 t.	ground cinnamon	5 mL
1 t.	ground nutmeg	5 mL
¼ t.	ground cloves	½ mL

*Unsweetened dried fruit can be bought at most health-food stores.

Base: Sift together flour, baking soda, and salt. Set aside. Cream together margarine, sugar replacement, and fructose. Add egg yolk and blend well. Gradually sift flour mixture into creamed mixture, mixing well. (Mixture will form crumbs.) Press mixture into the bottom of a 13 × 9 in. (33 × 23 cm) shiny baking pan.

Filling: Cut dried fruit into small pieces for good distribution. Set aside. In a bowl, slightly beat egg white with a fork. Add vanilla extract, sugar replacement, spices, and dried fruit. Mix well. Spread fruit mixture over base. Bake at 350°F (175°C) for 20 to 25 minutes, or until filling is set. Cool on rack. Cut into 48 bars.

Yield: 48 bars
Exchange, 1 bar: ⅓ bread
Calories, 1 bar: 25
Carbohydrates, 1 bar: 3 g

Pineapple Goody Bars

Filling:

8-oz. can	crushed pineapple in juice	227-g can
3 T.	white grape-juice concentrate	45 mL
1 T.	granulated sugar replacement	15 mL
1 T.	cornstarch	15 mL
1 t.	pineapple flavoring	5 mL
1 drop	yellow food coloring	1 drop

Base:

½ c.	quick-cooking oatmeal	125 mL
½ c.	all-purpose flour	125 mL
¼ c.	margarine	60 mL
1	egg white	1

Filling: Combine pineapple with juice, grape-juice concentrate, sugar replacement, and cornstarch. Stir to thoroughly dissolve cornstarch. Place over medium heat, and cook until mixture comes to a full boil, stirring constantly. Boil until mixture is thick and clear. Remove from heat. Stir in pineapple flavoring and food coloring. Set aside to cool

Base: Combine oatmeal, flour, margarine, and egg white in a bowl. Work into a dough. Lightly grease an 8 × 8 in. (20 × 20 cm) baking pan with vegetable-oil spray. Press mixture into the bottom of the pan. Bake at 350°F (175°C) for 10 minutes. Remove from oven. Pour and spread pineapple mixture over the entire surface of the base. Return to oven and bake for 25 minutes, or until filling is set. Cool on rack. Cut into 36 bars.

Yield: 36 bars
Exchange, 1 bar: ⅓ bread
Calories, 1 bar: 25
Carbohydrates, 1 bar: 4 g

Hank Bars

Base:

½ c.	quick-cooking oatmeal	125 mL
½ c.	all-purpose flour	125 mL
¼ c.	margarine	60 mL
1 t.	vanilla extract	5 mL

Topping:

½ c.	chocolate chips	125 mL
½ c.	chunky peanut butter	125 mL

Base: Combine oatmeal, flour, margarine, and vanilla in a mixing bowl. Cut and work margarine into dry mixture until mixture is in small crumbs. Lightly grease an 8 × 8 in. (20 × 20 cm) baking pan with vegetable-oil spray. Press mixture into the bottom of the pan. Bake at 350°F (175°C) for 15 to 20 minutes, or until lightly browned on edges. Remove from oven. Cool dough slightly.

Topping: Melt chocolate chips and peanut butter together in a saucepan over low heat. Spread chocolate mixture over entire surface of base. Cool completely; then cut into 36 bars.

Yield: 36 bars
Exchange, 1 bar: ¼ bread, ¼ fat
Calories, 1 bar: 56
Carbohydrates, 1 bar: 2 g

Butterscotch Bars

¼ c.	margarine	60 mL
⅔ c.	granulated brown-sugar replacement	180 mL
⅓ c.	granulated fructose	90 mL
1	egg	1
1 t.	vanilla extract	5 mL
1 c.	all-purpose flour	250 mL
¼ c.	chopped pecans	60 mL

Melt margarine over low heat in a medium-size saucepan. Remove from heat, and stir in brown-sugar replacement and fructose. Stir in egg and vanilla extract until well blended. Add flour and pecans. Stir until thoroughly blended. Spread batter evenly over the bottom of a greased 8-in. (20-cm) baking pan. Bake at 375°F (190°C) for 20 to 25 minutes, or until golden brown. Allow to cool in pan. Cut into 16 bars.

Yield: 16 bars
Exchange, 1 bar: ½ bread, ¾ fat
Calories, 1 bar: 72
Carbohydrates, 1 bar: 7 g

Apricot Bars

Filling:

16-oz. can	apricot halves in juice	454-g can
1 T.	white grape-juice concentrate	15 mL
2 T.	granulated sugar replacement	30 mL
1 T.	cornstarch	15 mL
1 t.	almond flavoring	5 mL
1 drop	red food coloring	1 drop
1 drop	yellow food coloring	1 drop

Base:

½ c.	quick-cooking oatmeal	125 mL
½ c.	all-purpose flour	125 mL
¼ c.	margarine	60 mL

Filling: Drain ½ c. (125 mL) of the juice from the apricots into a small saucepan. Thoroughly drain remaining apricots. Reserve apricot halves. Add grape-juice concentrate, sugar replacement, and cornstarch to saucepan. Stir to thoroughly dissolve cornstarch. Place over medium heat, and cook until mixture comes to a full boil, stirring constantly. Boil for 5 minutes, stirring constantly. Remove from heat. Add almond flavoring and food coloring. Set aside to cool.

Base: Combine oatmeal, flour, and margarine in a bowl. Cut and work margarine into dry mixture until mixture is in small crumbs. Lightly grease an 8 × 8 in. (20 × 20 cm) baking pan with vegetable-oil spray. Press mixture into the bottom of the pan. Bake at 350°F (175°C) for 10 minutes. Remove from oven. Place apricot halves over entire surface of base. Pour apricot filling over surface. Return to oven, and bake for 35 minutes or until filling is set. Cool on rack. Cut into 36 bars.

Yield: 36 bars
Exchange, 1 bar: ⅓ fruit, ¼ fat
Calories, 1 bar: 29
Carbohydrates, 1 bar: 4 g

Old-Fashioned Apple Bars

1 c.	all-purpose flour	250 mL
1 t.	baking powder	5 mL
1 t.	ground cinnamon	5 mL

½ t.	baking soda	2 mL
½ t.	ground nutmeg	2 mL
¼ t.	ground cloves	1 mL
⅔ c.	margarine	165 mL
½ c.	granulated sugar replacement	125 mL
¼ c.	granulated fructose	60 mL
2	eggs	2
1 c.	diced pared apples	250 mL
¾ c.	quick-cooking oatmeal	190 mL
⅓ c.	chopped walnuts	90 mL

Sift together flour, baking powder, cinnamon, baking soda, nutmeg, and cloves; set aside. Cream margarine, sugar replacement, and fructose in a mixing bowl, using and electric mixer at MEDIUM speed. Add eggs, one at a time, beating well after each addition. Gradually add dry ingredients to creamed mixture, beating well after each addition, using an electric mixer at LOW speed. Stir in diced apples, oatmeal, and walnuts. Spread batter into a greased 9 × 13 in. (23 × 33 cm) baking pan. Bake at 350°F (175°C) for 25 to 30 minutes or until top springs back when touched. Cool in pan on rack. Cut into 48 bars.

Yield: 48 bars
Exchange, 1 bar: ¼ bread, ½ fat
Calories, 1 bar: 46
Carbohydrates, 1 bar: 3 g

Carrot Bars

8 oz.	carrot cake mix, fructose-sweetened	227 g
¼ c.	grated carrots	60 mL
2 T.	pineapple juice	30 mL

Combine ingredients in a small bowl. Using a fork, blend ingredients together thoroughly. Allow to sit for 10 minutes at room temperature. Blend again. Spread mixture into a greased 8 × 8 in. (20 × 20 cm) baking pan. Bake at 350°F (175°C) for 15 to 17 minutes. Allow to cool in pan. Cut into 28 bars.

Yield: 28 bars
Exchange, 1 bar: ½ bread, ½ fat
Calories, 1 bar: 49
Carbohydrates, 1 bar: 8 g

Carrot Date Bars

8 oz.	carrot cake mix, fructose-sweetened	227 g
¼ c.	grated carrots	60 mL
1 T.	light sour cream	15 mL
2 T.	orange juice	30 mL
⅓ c.	finely chopped dates	90 mL

Combine cake mix, carrots, sour cream, and orange juice in a small bowl. Using a fork, blend ingredients together thoroughly. Allow to sit for 10 minutes at room temperature. Blend again. Stir in dates. Spread mixture into a greased 8 × 8 in. (20 × 20 cm) baking pan. Bake at 350°F (175°C) for 15 to 17 minutes. Allow to cool in pan. Cut into 28 bars.

Yield: 28 bars
Exchange, 1 bar: ½ bread, ¼ fruit
Calories, 1 bar: 53
Carbohydrates, 1 bar: 12 g

Banana Oat-Bran Squares

2	very ripe bananas	2
1	egg, slightly beaten	1
3 T.	granulated sugar replacement	45 mL
1 t.	vanilla extract	5 mL
½ c.	all-purpose flour	125 mL
1 c.	oat-bran flour	250 mL
1 t.	baking powder	5 mL
¼ t.	baking soda	1 mL
⅓ c.	coarsely chopped walnuts	90 mL

Slightly whip bananas in a bowl. Add beaten egg, sugar replacement, and vanilla. Beat just until blended. Stir in flours, baking powder, and baking soda thoroughly. Spray a 9 × 9 in. (23 × 23 cm) baking pan with vegetable-oil spray. Spread batter into the bottom of the pan. Sprinkle with the walnuts. Bake at 350°F (175°C) for 18 to 25 minutes or until toothpick inserted in middle comes out clean. Remove from oven, cool on rack, and cut into 36 squares.

Yield: 36 squares
Exchange, 1 square: ⅓ bread
Calories, 1 square: 23
Carbohydrates, 1 square: 5 g

Popular Raspberry Bars

½ c.	margarine	125 mL
¼ c.	granulated sugar replacement	60 mL
¼ c.	granulated fructose	60 mL
1 t.	almond flavoring	5 mL
1	egg	1
1 c.	all-purpose flour	250 mL
½ c.	quick-cooking oatmeal	125 mL
½ t.	baking powder	2 mL
dash each	salt and ground cloves	dash each
½ c.	all-fruit raspberry preserves	125 mL

Beat margarine, sugar replacement, and fructose together until well blended. Beat in almond flavoring and egg. Mix together flour, oatmeal, baking powder, salt, and cloves. Stir into creamed mixture. Spread half of the mixture on the bottom of a greased 9 × 9 in. (23 × 23 cm) baking pan. Spread with the raspberry preserves. Drop remaining batter by tea-spoonsful onto the top of the preserves. Bake at 350°F (175°C) for 25 minutes. Cut into 36 bars. Serve warm.

Yield: 36 bars
Exchange, 1 bar: ⅓ bread, ½ fat
Calories, 1 bar: 46
Carbohydrates, 1 bar: 5 g

Yogurt-Brownie Bars

8-oz. pkg.	brownie mix, fructose-sweetened	227-g pkg.
3 T.	low-fat plain yogurt	45 mL
½ t.	vanilla extract	2 mL
1	egg white	1

Combine brownie mix, yogurt, vanilla, and egg white in a bowl. Stir to mix thoroughly. Spread evenly in the bottom of a 9 × 9 in. (23 × 23 cm) baking pan. Bake at 350°F (175°C) for 20 to 25 minutes. Allow to cool in pan. Cut into 36 bars.

Yield: 36 bars
Exchange, 1 bar: ½ bread, ½ fat
Calories, 1 bar: 50
Carbohydrates, 1 bar: 8 g

White-Raisin–Filled Bars

Base:

1 c.	all-purpose flour	250 mL
1 c.	quick-cooking oatmeal	250 mL
⅔ c.	granulated brown-sugar replacement	165 mL
¼ t.	baking soda	1 mL
½ c.	margarine	125 mL

Filling:

½ c.	cold water	125 mL
2 t.	cornstarch	10 mL
1 c.	white raisins	250 mL

Base: Combine flour, oatmeal, brown-sugar replacement, and baking soda in a mixing bowl. Cut or work margarine into mixture until mixture is coarse crumbs. Reserve ½ c. (125 mL), and set aside for topping. Press remaining mixture into the bottom of an ungreased 9 × 9 in. (23 × 23 cm) baking pan.

Filling: Combine cold water and cornstarch in a saucepan. Stir to dissolve cornstarch thoroughly Add raisins. Cook and stir over medium heat until mixture is very thick and bubbly. Pour over base in baking pan. Sprinkle with reserved base. Bake at 350°F (175°C) for 30 to 35 minutes, or until the top is golden and the filling is set. Cool in pan on rack. Cut into 36 bars.

Yield: 36 bars
Exchange, 1 bar: ⅓ bread, ⅓ fruit
Calories, 1 bar: 48
Carbohydrates, 1 bar: 7 g

Caramel-Flavored Bars

1 c.	all-purpose flour	250 mL
1 t.	baking powder	5 mL
dash	salt	dash
¼ c.	margarine	60 mL
½ c.	granulated brown-sugar replacement	125 mL
¼ c.	granulated fructose	60 mL
1	egg	1
1 t.	caramel flavoring	5 mL
½ t.	burnt-sugar flavoring	2 mL

| ½ t. | vanilla extract | 2 mL |
| ¼ c. | finely chopped walnuts | 60 mL |

Sift together flour, baking powder, and salt; set aside. Combine margarine, brown-sugar replacement, and fructose in a mixing bowl. Stir to blend thoroughly. Add egg, flavorings, and vanilla extract; mix well. Gradually stir flour mixture into margarine mixture. Stir in walnuts. Spread mixture into the bottom of a greased 8 × 8 in. (20 × 20 cm) baking pan. Bake at 350°F (175°C) for 30 minutes, or until top springs back when touched. Cool in pan on rack. Cut into 36 bars.

Yield: 36 bars
Exchange, 1 bar: ¼ bread, ¼ fat
Calories, 1 bar: 29
Carbohydrates, 1 bar: 3 g

Granola Bars

1 c.	low-fat granola	250 mL
1 c.	quick-cooking oatmeal	250 mL
½ c.	all-purpose flour	125 mL
1	large egg	1
1	egg white	1
¼ c.	liquid fructose	60 mL
⅓ c.	cooking oil	90 mL
3 T.	granulated brown-sugar replacement	45 mL

Combine granola, oatmeal, and flour in a mixing bowl. Stir to blend. Combine egg and egg white in a small bowl or cup. Beat until well blended. Pour into cereal mixture. Add liquid fructose, cooking oil, and brown-sugar replacement. Stir thoroughly until the mixture is completely coated with liquid. Completely line an 8 × 8 in. (20 × 20 cm) baking pan with foil. (You'll use this foil to remove cookie mixture from pan.) Grease foil with a vegetable-oil spray. Press cookie mixture into the bottom of the pan. Bake at 325°F (165°C) for 30 to 35 minutes, or until lightly browned around the edges. Remove pan from oven. Remove foil with cookie mixture from pan to a rack. Cool. Cut into 25 bars.

Yield: 25 bars
Exchange, 1 bar: ⅔ bread
Calories, 1 bar: 47
Carbohydrates, 1 bar: 9 g

Lemon-Cream Bars

Base:

⅓ c.	margarine	90 mL
2 T.	granulated sugar replacement	30 mL
1 c.	all-purpose flour	250 mL

Filling:

2	eggs	2
2 T.	all-purpose flour	30 mL
¼ c.	granulated fructose	60 mL
3 T.	granulated sugar replacement	45 mL
3 T	fresh lemon juice	45 mL
2 t.	finely shredded lemon peel	10 mL
¼ t.	baking powder	2 mL

Base: Combine margarine and sugar replacement in a mixing bowl. Beat to blend. Beat in flour until mixture is crumbly. Press into the bottom of an 8 × 8 in. (20 × 20 cm) baking pan. Bake at 350°F (175°C) for 15 to 17 minutes, or until lightly browned. Remove from oven.

Filling: Combine eggs, flour, fructose, sugar replacement, lemon juice, lemon peel, and baking powder in a mixing bowl. Beat for 2 minutes. Pour over base layer. Return to oven, and bake about 20 minutes more, or until set. Cool on rack. Cut into 25 bars.

Yield: 25 bars
Exchange, 1 bar: ⅓ bread, ½ fat
Calories, 1 bar: 48
Carbohydrates, 1 bar: 4 g

Prune Bars

¼ c.	margarine	60 mL
1 c.	all-purpose flour	250 mL
½ t.	ground cinnamon	2 mL
2 T	granulated fructose	30 mL
2 T.	granulated sugar replacement	30 mL
½ c.	orange juice	125 mL
1	egg	1
½ t.	baking powder	2 mL
¼ t.	baking soda	1 mL
½ c.	snipped dried pitted prunes	125 mL

Beat margarine with an electric mixer on HIGH for 30 seconds. Add ½ c. (125 mL) of the flour, cinnamon, fructose, sugar replacement, ¼ c. (60 mL) of the orange juice, egg, baking powder, and baking soda; then continue beating for 1 minute more, or until thoroughly blended. Beat in remaining ½ c. (125 mL) of flour and remaining orange juice. Stir in snipped prunes. Spread cookie batter into the bottom of a 7 × 11 in. (17 × 27 cm) ungreased baking pan. Bake at 350°F (175°C) for 25 minutes, or until toothpick inserted in middle comes out clean. Cool on rack. Cut into 40 bars.

Yield: 40 bars
Exchange, 1 bar: ⅓ bread, ¼ fat
Calories, 1 bar: 30
Carbohydrates, 1 bar: 3 g

Apple Date Bars

¼ c.	margarine	60 mL
1 c.	all-purpose flour	250 mL
2 T.	granulated fructose	30 mL
2 T.	granulated sugar replacement	30 mL
½ c.	apple-juice concentrate	125 mL
1	egg	1
½ t.	baking powder	2 mL
¼ t.	baking soda	1 mL
½ c.	chopped pitted dates	125 mL

Beat margarine with an electric mixer on HIGH for 30 seconds. Add ½ c. (125 mL) of the flour, fructose, sugar replacement, ¼ c. (60 mL) of the apple-juice concentrate, egg, baking powder, and baking soda; then continue beating for 1 minute more, or until thoroughly blended. Beat in remaining ½ c. (125 mL) of flour and remaining apple-juice concentrate. Stir in dates. Spread cookie batter into the bottom of a 7 × 11 in. (17 × 27 cm) ungreased baking pan. Bake at 350°F (175°C) for 25 minutes, or until toothpick inserted in middle comes out clean. Cool on rack. Cut into 40 bars.

Yield: 40 bars
Exchange, 1 bar: ⅓ bread, ¼ fat
Calories, 1 bar: 31
Carbohydrates, 1 bar: 3 g

Chocolate & Vanilla-Layered Bars

1½ c.	all-purpose flour	375 mL
¼ t.	salt	1 mL
¾ c.	margarine	190 mL
¾ c.	granulated sugar replacement	190 mL
⅓ c.	granulated fructose	90 mL
3	eggs	3
1 t.	vanilla extract	5 mL
1½ oz.	unsweetened chocolate, melted and cooled	43 g

Sift together flour and salt; set aside. Beat margarine, sugar replacement, and fructose until creamy. Add eggs, one at a time, beating well after each addition. Beat in vanilla. Gradually stir flour mixture into creamed mixture. Blend well. Spread two-thirds of the batter on the bottom of a greased 9-in. (23-cm) baking pan. Stir melted chocolate into the remaining cookie batter. Spread chocolate batter evenly over vanilla batter. Bake at 350°F (175°C) for 35 minutes, or until toothpick inserted in middle comes out clean. Allow to cool in pan. Cut into 36 bars.

Yield: 36 bars
Exchange, 1 bar: ⅓ bread, ½ fat
Calories, 1 bar: 46
Carbohydrates, 1 bar: 5 g

Maple Walnut Bars

1½ c.	all-purpose flour	375 mL
¼ c.	granulated brown-sugar replacement	60 mL
½ c.	margarine	125 mL
1 c.	dietetic maple syrup	250 mL
2	eggs	2
½ t.	vanilla extract	2 mL
2 T.	all-purpose flour	30 mL
dash	salt	dash
⅓ c.	chopped walnuts	90 mL

Combine the 1½ c. (375 mL) of flour, brown-sugar replacement, and margarine in a mixing bowl. Using a pastry blender, a fork, or your fingers, work the dough into crumbs. Press the crumbs into the bottom of a greased 13 × 9 in. (33 × 23 cm) baking pan. Bake at 350°F (175°C) for 15 minutes. Heat maple syrup until warm. Beat eggs in a bowl. Slowly pour the hot maple syrup into the beaten egg, stirring constantly. Stir in vanilla, the 2 T. (30 mL) of flour, and salt. Blend thoroughly. Pour over baked crust. Sprinkle with walnuts. Return to oven, and bake 15 or 20 minutes more. Allow to cool in pan. Cut into 54 bars.

Yield: 54 bars
Exchange, 1 bar: ¼ bread, ½ fat
Calories, 1 bar: 40
Carbohydrates, 1 bar: 3 g

Linear Walnut Bars

¾ c.	margarine	190 mL
⅓ c.	granulated sugar replacement	90 mL
2 T.	granulated fructose	30 mL
1	egg	1
½ t.	freshly grated lemon peel	2 mL
½ t.	ground cinnamon	2 mL
⅛ t.	ground cloves	0.5 mL
2 c.	all-purpose flour	500 mL
1 c.	all-fruit raspberry preserves	250 mL

Using an electric mixer on MEDIUM, beat together margarine, sugar replacement, fructose, egg, lemon peel, cinnamon, and cloves. Blend in flour. Reserve about one-fourth of the cookie dough. Push remaining dough into the bottom and about ½ in. (1.25 cm) up the sides of a greased 9 × 9 in. (23 × 23 cm) baking pan. Spread raspberry preserves evenly over the top of the dough. Make small snakelike strips using reserved dough by rolling small amounts of dough along a floured board with the palms of your hands. Arrange these strips in a lattice pattern over the top of the raspberry preserves. Press the ends of the strips into the dough on the sides of the pan. Bake at 325°F (165°C) for 40 to 45 minutes, or until lightly browned. Cool in pan. Cut into 36 bars.

Yield: 36 bars
Exchange, 1 bar: ¼ bread, ½ fat
Calories, 1 bar: 41
Carbohydrates, 1 bar: 4 g

Peanut-Butter Crisp-Rice Bars

⅓ c.	liquid fructose sweetener	90 mL
2 T.	granulated brown-sugar replacement	30 mL
1 c.	peanut butter	250 mL
¾ t.	vanilla extract	4 mL
4 c.	crisp-rice cereal	1000 mL

Combine liquid fructose and brown-sugar replacement in a large sauce-pan. Bring to a boil. Remove saucepan from heat, and add peanut butter and vanilla extract. Stir until peanut butter is melted. Stir in the crisp-rice cereal. Press into the bottom of an ungreased 9 × 9 in. (23 × 23 cm) baking pan. Chill at least 1 hour, or until firm. Remove from pan. Cut into 36 bars.

Yield: 36 bars
Exchange, 1 bar: 1 fat
Calories, 1 bar: 47
Carbohydrates, 1 bar: 1 g

Peanut-Butter Oatmeal Bars

¾ c.	chunky peanut butter	190 mL
¾ c.	granulated sugar replacement	190 mL
¼ c.	reduced-calorie margarine	60 mL
¼ c.	liquid fructose	60 mL
1	egg	1
1 t.	vanilla extract	5 mL
1 c.	quick-cooking oatmeal	250 mL
1 c.	uncooked oat bran	250 mL
½ c.	nonfat dry milk	125 mL

Combine peanut butter, sugar replacement, and margarine in a mixing bowl. Beat to blend thoroughly. Beat in liquid fructose, egg, and vanilla extract. Stir in oatmeal, oat bran, and dry milk. Turn batter into a greased 13 × 9 in. (33 × 23 cm) baking pan. Bake at 350°F (175°C) for 30 to 35 minutes, or until top has browned and toothpick inserted in middle comes out clean. Cool. Cut into 32 bars.

Yield: 32 bars
Exchange, 1 bar: ½ bread, ¾ fat
Calories, 1 bar: 64
Carbohydrates, 1 bar: 7 g

Salted-Peanut Brownie Bars

8.5-oz. pkg.	brownie mix, fructose-sweetened	241-g pkg.
⅓ c.	water	90 mL
1	egg	1
½ c.	salted peanuts	125 mL

Combine brownie mix, water, and egg in a bowl. Blend by hand until smooth. Chop peanuts into small pieces. Stir nuts into mix. Spread batter into a greased 8-in. (20-cm) square baking pan. Bake at 350°F (175°C) for 25 to 30 minutes, or until toothpick inserted in middle comes out clean. Cool. Cut into 16 bars.

Yield: 16 bars
Exchange, 1 bar: ½ bread, 1 fat
Calories, 1 bar: 71
Carbohydrates, 1 bar: 8 g

Applesauce Bars for a Crowd

2 c.	all-purpose flour	500 mL
½ c.	granulated sugar replacement	125 mL
¼ c.	granulated fructose	60 mL
2 t.	baking powder	10 mL
2 t.	ground cinnamon	10 mL
1 t.	baking soda	5 mL
¼ t.	ground cloves	1 mL
dash	salt	dash
4	eggs, beaten	4
16-oz. can	unsweetened applesauce	454-g can
1 c.	cooking oil	250 mL

Combine flour, sugar replacement, fructose, baking powder, cinnamon, baking soda, cloves, and salt in a mixing bowl. Stir in eggs, applesauce, and cooking oil. Spread cookie batter into an ungreased 10 × 15 in. (25 × 39 cm) shiny jelly-roll pan. Bake at 350°F (175°C) for 25 to 30 minutes, or until toothpick inserted in middle comes out clean. Cool on racks. Cut into 70 bars.

Yield: 70 bars
Exchange, 1 bar: ⅓ bread, ¼ fat
Calories, 1 bar: 45
Carbohydrates, 1 bar: 4 g

Pumpkin Bars for a Crowd

2 c.	all-purpose flour	500 mL
½ c.	granulated sugar replacement	125 mL
¼ c.	granulated fructose	60 mL
2 t.	baking powder	10 mL
2 t.	ground cinnamon	10 mL
1 t.	baking soda	5 mL
¼ t.	ground cloves	1 mL
4	eggs, beaten	4
16-oz. can	pumpkin purée	454-g can
1 c.	cooking oil	250 mL

Combine flour, sugar replacement, fructose, baking powder, cinnamon, baking soda, and cloves in a mixing bowl. Stir in eggs, pumpkin purée, and cooking oil. Spread cookie batter into an ungreased 10 × 15 in. (25 × 39 cm) shiny jelly-roll pan. Bake at 350°F (175°C) for 25 to 30 minutes, or until toothpick inserted in middle comes out clean. Cool on rack. Cut into 70 bars.

Yield: 70 bars
Exchange, 1 bar: ⅓ bread, ¼ fat
Calories, 1 bar: 46
Carbohydrates, 1 bar: 4 g

Chocolate-Cake Brownies for a Crowd

4	egg whites	4
½ t.	cream of tartar	2 mL
3 T.	granulated sugar replacement	45 mL
4	egg yolks	4
¾ c.	low-fat milk	190 mL
1 t.	vanilla extract	5 mL
¼ t.	brandy flavoring	1 mL
¾ c.	all-purpose flour	190 mL
⅓ c.	unsweetened baking cocoa	90 mL
3 T.	granulated sugar replacement	45 mL
1 t.	baking powder	5 mL
½ t.	baking soda	2 mL
dash	salt	dash

Using an electric mixer, beat egg whites and cream of tartar at HIGH speed until foamy, about 5 minutes. Beat in 3 T. (45 mL) of sugar replacement. Continue beating until stiff peaks form. Set aside. Beat egg yolks until thick and lemon-colored. Beat in milk, vanilla extract, and brandy flavoring. At LOW speed, beat in flour, cocoa, 3 T. (45 mL) sugar replacement, baking powder, baking soda, and salt into egg-yolk mixture. Using MEDIUM speed, beat mixture for 2 minutes. Pour egg-yolk mixture over egg-white mixture; carefully fold by hand until evenly blended. Spray a 15 × 10 in. (39 × 25 cm) jelly-roll pan with vegetable-oil spray. Pour batter into jelly-roll pan. Bake at 350°F (175°C) for 7 to 10 minutes, or until toothpick inserted in middle come out clean. Remove from oven, and cool on rack. If desired, frost with 1 box of frosting mix, noting calorie change. Cut into 50 brownies.

Yield: 50 brownies
Exchange, 1 brownie: ⅓ bread
Calories, 1 brownie: 21
Carbohydrates, 1 brownie: 3 g

Yield: 50 brownies
Exchange, 1 brownie with frosting: ⅓ bread
Calories, 1 brownie with frosting: 27
Carbohydrates, 1 brownie with frosting: 3 g

Chocolate-Frosted Brownies

| 8.5-oz. box | brownie mix, fructose-sweetened | 241-g box |
| ¼ c. | mini chocolate chips | 60 mL |

Prepare brownie mix as directed on box. When brownies are taken from oven, sprinkle chocolate chips over the top, allowing chips to warm. Using a kitchen table knife, spread softened chocolate chips evenly over surface. Allow to cool in pan for 3 to 4 minutes more. Cover with aluminum foil, and cool completely. Cut into 16 brownies

Yield: 16 brownies
Exchange, 1 brownie: ½ bread, ¾ fat
Calories, 1 brownie: 60
Carbohydrates, 1 brownie: 8 g

Buttermilk Brownies

2 c.	all-purpose flour	500 mL
¼ c.	granulated fructose	60 mL
¼ c.	granulated sugar replacement	60 mL
1 t.	baking soda	5 mL
dash	salt	dash
¾ c.	margarine	190 mL
1 c.	water	250 mL
⅓ c.	unsweetened baking cocoa	90 mL
2	eggs	2
½ c.	buttermilk	125 mL
2 t.	vanilla extract	10 mL

Combine flour, fructose, sugar replacement, baking soda, and salt in a mixing bowl. Combine margarine, water, and cocoa in a saucepan. Cook and stir over medium heat until mixture begins to boil. Remove from heat. Pour chocolate mixture into flour mixture. Using an electric mixer, beat batter until thoroughly blended. Add eggs, buttermilk, and vanilla extract. Beat for 1 minute. Grease and flour a 15 × 10 in. (39 × 25 cm) jelly-roll pan. Pour batter into pan, and spread evenly on the bottom. Bake at 350°F (175°C) for 25 minutes, or until toothpick inserted in middle comes out clean. Cut into 50 brownies.

Yield: 50 brownies
Exchange, 1 brownie: ¼ bread, ⅓ fat
Calories, 1 brownie: 51
Carbohydrates, 1 brownie: 4 g

Gingerbread Bars

1 c.	all-purpose flour	250 mL
¾ c.	whole-wheat flour	190 mL
⅔ c.	granulated sugar replacement	180 mL
1 T.	baking powder	15 mL
½ t.	ground ginger	2 mL
¼ t.	salt	1 mL
¼ t.	ground cloves	1 mL
2	eggs	2
⅔ c.	low-fat milk	180 mL
¼ c.	cooking oil	60 mL
3 T.	molasses*	45 mL

Combine flours, sugar replacement, baking powder, ginger, salt, and cloves in a mixing bowl. Stir to mix. Add eggs, milk, and oil. Beat to blend thoroughly. Beat in molasses. Beat 1 to 2 minutes more. Pour into a greased 13 × 9 in. (33 × 23 cm) baking pan. Bake at 350°F (175°C) for 25 to 30 minutes, or until toothpick inserted in middle comes out clean. Cool. Cut into 32 bars.

*Because the recipe for these bars calls for molasses, check with your doctor or dietician before baking or eating this dessert.

Yield: 32 bars
Exchange, 1 bar: ⅓ bread, ⅓ fat
Calories, 1 bar: 47
Carbohydrates, 1 bar: 5 g

Orange Oat Bars

1 c.	quick-cooking oatmeal	250 mL
1 c.	orange juice	250 mL
2 c.	uncooked oat bran	500 mL
⅔ c.	all-purpose flour	180 mL
½ c.	nonfat dry milk	125 mL
2 t.	baking powder	10 mL
½ t.	baking soda	2 mL
dash	salt	dash
⅓ c.	granulated sugar replacement	90 mL
⅓ c.	granulated fructose	90 mL
¼ c.	vegetable oil	60 mL
2	eggs	2
2 t.	vanilla extract	10 mL

Soak oatmeal in orange juice in a large bowl for at least 15 minutes. Combine oat bran, flour, dry milk, baking powder, baking soda, and salt in a large mixing bowl. Stir sugar replacement, fructose, oil, eggs, and vanilla into the soaked oatmeal. Then stir oat bran–flour mixture into the oatmeal mixture. Turn into a greased 13 × 9 in. (33 × 23 cm) baking pan. Bake at 425°F (220°C) for 25 to 35 minutes, or until a toothpick inserted in middle comes out clean. Cool. Cut into 54 bars.

Yield: 54 bars
Exchange, 1 bar: ½ bread, ¼ fat
Calories, 1 bar: 47
Carbohydrates, 1 bar: 7 g

Bars—Four Variations

Base:

1 c.	soft margarine	250 mL
⅔ c.	granulated brown-sugar replacement	190 mL
⅓ c.	granulated fructose	90 mL
1	egg	1
3 t.	vanilla extract	15 mL
2 c.	all-purpose flour	500 mL
3 T.	semisweet chocolate chips	45 mL

Topping 1:

¼ c.	semisweet chocolate chips	60 mL

Topping 2:

3 T.	grated dietetic white chocolate	45 mL
2 T.	finely chopped pecans	30 mL

Topping 3:

⅓ c.	creamy peanut butter	90 mL
2 T.	finely chopped walnuts	30 mL

Topping 4:

¼ c.	all-fruit raspberry preserves	60 mL

Using an electric mixer, cream margarine in a large mixing bowl. Add brown-sugar replacement and fructose. Beat well. Beat in egg and vanilla extract. Add flour, 1 c. (250 mL) at a time, beating well after each addition. Transfer half of the mixture to a 15 × 10 in. (39 × 25 cm) jelly-roll pan. Spread with a knife or use a floured pasta roller to roll dough evenly into half of the pan crosswise. Melt the 3 T. (45 mL) of chocolate chips. Stir or beat into remaining dough. Spread with a knife, or use a floured pasta roller to roll dough evenly into remaining half of pan. Bake at 350°F (175°C) for 15 minutes. Sprinkle the ¼ c. (60 mL) of chocolate chips on half of the chocolate dough. Sprinkle the grated white chocolate on half of the white dough (pecans will be added later). Spread peanut butter on remaining half of chocolate dough; sprinkle with chopped walnuts. Spread the all-fruit preserves on the remaining half of the white dough. Spread the now-warmed and melted chocolate chips to cover its dough. Spread the now-warmed and melted white chocolate to cover its dough; sprinkle the white chocolate with the chopped pecans. Return pan to oven, and bake for 5 minutes more. Cool in pan on rack. Cut into bars.

Yield for chocolate dough with chocolate chips: 50 bars
Exchange, 1 bar: ⅓ bread, ¾ fat
Calories, 1 bar: 49
Carbohydrates, 1 bar: 4 g

Yield for chocolate dough with peanut butter: 50 bars
Exchange, 1 bar: ⅓ bread, 1 fat
Calories, 1 bar: 51
Carbohydrates, 1 bar: 4 g

Yield for white dough with white chocolate: 50 bars
Exchange, 1 bar: ⅓ bread, ¾ fat
Calories, 1 bar: 47
Carbohydrates, 1 bar: 4 g

Yield for white dough with preserves: 50 bars
Exchange, 1 bar: ⅓ bread, ¾ fat
Calories, 1 bar: 45
Carbohydrates, 1 bar: 4 g

Chocolate Cereal Bars

¼ c.	liquid fructose	60 mL
3 T.	granulated sugar replacement	45 mL
2 oz.	semisweet baking chocolate	57 g
4 c.	cornflakes	1000 mL

Combine liquid fructose, sugar replacement, and semisweet baking chocolate in a large saucepan. Bring to a boil. Remove saucepan from heat. Measure the cornflakes in a large measuring cup. Crush flakes until measurement is reduced to 2 cups (500 mL). Stir crushed flakes into the chocolate mixture. Press mixture into the bottom of an ungreased 8 × 8 in. (20 × 20 cm) baking pan. Chill at least 1 hour, or until firm. Remove from pan. Cut into 25 bars.

Yield: 25 bars
Exchange, 1 bar: ⅓ bread, ¼ fat
Calories, 1 bar: 36
Carbohydrates, 1 bar: 4 g

Chocolate Cream-Cheese Bars

Cream-cheese mixture:

2 T.	margarine	30 mL
3 oz.	cream cheese	85 g
3 T.	granulated sugar replacement	45 mL
1	egg	1
1 T.	all-purpose flour	15 mL
1 t.	vanilla extract	5 mL

Chocolate mixture:

3 oz.	semisweet chocolate	85 g
3 T.	margarine	45 mL
2	eggs	2
½ c.	granulated sugar replacement	125 mL
¼ c.	granulated fructose	60 mL
2 t.	vanilla extract	10 mL
½ c.	all-purpose flour	125 mL
½ t.	baking powder	2 mL

Cream-cheese mixture: Combine margarine and cream cheese in a mixing bowl. Beat until thoroughly blended. Add sugar replacement and egg. Beat until fluffy. Blend in flour and vanilla. Set aside.

Chocolate mixture: Melt chocolate and margarine in a small saucepan. Stir to blend, and allow to cool. Beat eggs on HIGH in an electric mixer, until lemon-colored. Beat in sugar replacement, fructose, and vanilla. Gradually add flour and baking powder, beating well after each addition. Blend in melted chocolate. Spread half of the chocolate mixture on the bottom of a greased 9-in. (23-cm) square baking pan. Pour cream-cheese mixture over the surface of the chocolate mixture. Cover with remaining chocolate mixture. Take a knife and swirl through all layers. Bake at 350°F (175°C) for 40 to 45 minutes, or until toothpick inserted in middle comes out clean. Cool. Cut into 36 bars.

Yield: 36 bars
Exchange, 1 bar: ¼ bread, ½ fat
Calories, 1 bar: 39
Carbohydrates, 1 bar: 3 g

Moulded, or Hand-Shaped, Cookies

Brownie Espresso-Cream Cookies

1 T.	margarine	15 mL
1 oz.	unsweetened baking chocolate	28 g
1 t.	instant espresso granules or powder	5 mL
2 T.	granulated sugar replacement	30 mL
1 T.	granulated fructose	15 mL
2	egg whites	2
½ t.	vanilla extract	2 mL
1 c.	all-purpose flour	250 mL
1 t.	baking powder	5 mL
2 t.	sugar-free chocolate powdered-drink mix	10 mL

Combine margarine, baking chocolate, and espresso powder in a medium-size microwavable mixing bowl. Microwave on HIGH for 1 minute, or until margarine and chocolate are melted. Stir to blend completely, and dissolve espresso powder. Set aside to cool slightly. Use a wire whisk to beat in sugar replacement, fructose, egg whites, and vanilla. Beat for 1 minute. Add flour and baking powder; stir until completely blended. Cover with plastic wrap, and refrigerate for at least 1 hour, or until needed. Form dough into small balls; then press balls into patties using the palm of your hand. Spray cookie sheet lightly with vegetable-oil spray. Place patties about 1 in. (2.5 cm) apart on the cookie sheet. Bake at 375°F (190°C) for 10 to 12 minutes. Remove from pan, and, while cookies are still hot, sprinkle with chocolate powdered-drink mix.

Yield: 24 cookies
Exchange, 1 cookie: ⅓ bread
Calories, 1 cookie: 24
Carbohydrates, 1 cookie: 4 g

Chocolate Doodles

¼ c.	margarine	60 mL
3 oz.	semisweet baking chocolate	85 g
1¾ c.	all-purpose flour	440 mL
1½ t.	baking powder	7 mL
¾ c.	granulated sugar replacement	190 mL
⅓ c.	granulated fructose	90 mL
3	eggs	3
2 t.	vanilla extract	10 mL

Combine margarine and baking chocolate in the top of a double boiler. Bring water to a boil, reduce heat to low, and heat until chocolate melts, stirring occasionally. Meanwhile, sift together the flour and baking powder. Remove double boiler from heat. Beat in the sugar replacement, fructose, and eggs. Add half of the flour mixture, and beat well. Remove the top half of the double boiler. Thoroughly stir in vanilla and remaining flour mixture. Cover and chill for at least 2 hours. Coat hands well with flour, and roll dough into 1-in. (2.5-cm) balls. Place balls on very lightly greased cookie sheet. Bake at 325°F (165°C) for 15 minutes. Move to cooling racks.

Yield: 60 cookies
Exchange, 1 cookie: ¼ bread, ¼ fat
Calories, 1 cookie: 32
Carbohydrates, 1 cookie: 4 g

Coconut Oatmeal Cookies

1 c.	all-purpose flour	250 mL
1 t.	baking soda	5 mL
¼ t.	salt	1 mL
1 c.	vegetable shortening, melted	250 mL
⅔ c.	granulated brown-sugar replacement	180 mL
⅓ c.	granulated fructose	90 mL
2	eggs	2
1 t.	vanilla extract	5 mL
½ c.	unsweetened flaked coconut	125 mL
2 c.	quick-cooking oatmeal	500 mL

Sift together flour, baking soda, and salt; set aside. Using an electric mixer, beat together melted shortening, brown-sugar replacement, and fructose. Add eggs, one at a time, beating well after each addition. Beat in vanilla. Stir flour mixture into creamed mixture until well mixed. Stir in coconut and oatmeal. Shape dough into 1-in. (2.5-cm) balls. Place on greased cookie sheet. Bake at 325°F (165°C) for 12 to 14 minutes, or until golden brown. Move to cooling racks.

Yield: 72 cookies
Exchange, 1 cookie: 1/3 bread, 1/4 fat
Calories, 1 cookie: 32
Carbohydrates, 1 cookie: 4 g

Cinnamon Cookies

1 c.	margarine	500 mL
2/3 c.	granulated sugar replacement	180 mL
1/3 c.	granulated fructose	90 mL
3	eggs	3
4 1/3 c.	all-purpose flour	1090 mL
2 t.	baking powder	10 mL
1/2 t.	baking soda	2 mL
1 t.	ground cinnamon	5 mL
2 T.	olive oil	30 mL
1	egg yolk, beaten	1

Beat margarine in a mixing bowl. Gradually add sugar replacement and fructose. Beat until fluffy. Add eggs, one at a time, beating well after each addition. Stir together flour, baking powder, baking soda, and cinnamon. Stir half of the flour mixture into the creamed mixture. Add olive oil and mix well. Add remaining flour mixture, and stir until well blended. Shape dough into balls, and place on a very lightly greased cookie sheet. Lightly brush top of each cookie with the beaten egg yolk. Bake at 350°F (175°C) for 20 minutes. Move to cooling racks.

Yield: 96 cookies
Exchange, 1 cookie: 1/3 bread
Calories, 1 cookie: 31
Carbohydrates, 1 cookie: 4 g

Cowboy Cookies

1 c.	all-purpose flour	250 mL
¾ t.	baking soda	4 mL
½ t.	baking powder	2 mL
½ c.	vegetable shortening	125 mL
¾ c.	granulated sugar replacement	190 mL
⅓ c.	granulated fructose	90 mL
1	egg	1
½ t.	vanilla extract	2 mL
¾ c.	quick-cooking oatmeal	190 mL
¾ c.	toasted-rice cereal	190 mL

Sift together flour, baking soda, and baking powder; set aside. Using an electric mixer, beat shortening, sugar replacement, and fructose until fluffy. Beat in egg and vanilla extract. Gradually stir flour mixture into creamed mixture. Stir in oatmeal and rice cereal. Form into 1-in. (2.5-cm) balls. Place balls on a greased cookie sheet. Bake at 350°F (175°C) for 15 minutes. Move to cooling rack.

Yield: 36 cookies
Exchange, 1 cookie: ⅓ bread
Calories, 1 cookie: 28
Carbohydrates, 1 cookie: 4 g

Brown-Sugar Oatmeal Coconut Cookies

½ c.	all-purpose flour	125 mL
½ t.	baking soda	2 mL
dash	salt	dash
½ c.	vegetable shortening, melted	125 mL
¾ c.	granulated brown-sugar replacement	190 mL
¼ c.	granulated fructose	60 mL
1	egg	1
½ t.	vanilla extract	2 mL
1 c.	quick-cooking oatmeal	250 mL
⅓ c.	unsweetened coconut	90 mL

Sift together flour, baking soda, and salt; set aside. Using an electric mixer, beat shortening, brown-sugar replacement, and fructose on MEDIUM until well blended. Add egg and beat well. Gradually stir flour mixture into creamed mixture. Stir in vanilla extract. Stir in oatmeal and coconut. Shape dough into balls, and place on greased cookie sheet. Bake at 325°F (165°C) for 12 to 15 minutes. Move to cooling racks.

Yield: 42 cookies
Exchange, 1 cookie: ¼ bread, ⅓ fat
Calories, 1 cookie: 40
Carbohydrates, 1 cookie: 3 g

Pfeffernuss

2	eggs	2
1 c.	granulated brown-sugar replacement	250 mL
½ c.	granulated fructose	125 mL
2 t.	fresh lemon juice	10 mL
2 c.	all-purpose flour	500 mL
2 t.	ground cinnamon	10 mL
½ t.	baking soda	2 mL
½ t.	ground cardamom	2 mL
½ t.	ground nutmeg	2 mL
½ t.	ground allspice	2 mL
½ t.	ground cloves	2 mL
¼ t.	salt	1 mL
¼ t.	ground black pepper	1 mL
¼ t.	ground blanched almonds	1 mL
	grated zest of one lemon	

Combine eggs, brown-sugar replacement, and fructose in a mixing bowl. Beat to blend for 10 full minutes. Beat in lemon juice. In a bowl, combine flour, cinnamon, baking soda, cardamom, nutmeg, allspice, cloves, salt, and black pepper. Stir to mix. Gradually add flour mixture to egg mixture. Beat well after each addition. Add almonds and lemon zest. Stir to mix. Shape dough into balls, and place them on greased cookie sheets. Allow the balls to "ripen" overnight at room temperature. Bake at 350°F (175°C) for 15 minutes, or until cracks form in the tops. Move to cooling racks.

Yield: 70 balls
Exchange, 1 ball: ⅓ bread
Calories, 1 ball: 21
Carbohydrates, 1 ball: 4 g

Old-Fashioned Brown-Sugar Cookies

2 c + 2 T.	all-purpose flour	530 mL
1 t.	baking soda	5 mL
1 t.	cream of tartar	5 mL
½ c.	margarine	125 mL
¾ c.	granulated brown-sugar replacement	190 mL
¼ c.	granulated fructose	60 mL
2 t.	caramel flavoring	10 mL
2 small	eggs	2 small

Sift together flour, baking soda, and cream of tartar; set aside. Using an electric mixer, beat together margarine, brown-sugar replacement, fructose, and caramel flavoring. Add eggs, one at a time, beating well after each addition. Stir flour mixture into creamed mixture, blending well. Shape dough into balls. Place balls on a greased cookie sheet. Dip a kitchen fork into flour, and flatten each cookie with the tines of the fork. Bake at 375°F (190°C) for 10 minutes. Move to cooling racks.

Yield: 42 cookies
Exchange, 1 cookie: ⅓ bread, ⅓ fat
Calories, 1 cookie: 42
Carbohydrates, 1 cookie: 5 g

Date Delights

½ c.	margarine	125 mL
3 T.	granulated sugar replacement	45 mL
1 T.	granulated fructose	15 mL
1 t.	vanilla extract	5 mL
1 c.	all-purpose flour	250 mL
¼ c.	finely chopped dates	60 mL

Using an electric mixer, beat margarine, sugar replacement, and fructose until light and fluffy. Beat in vanilla. Stir in flour. Fold in dates until well blended. Shape dough into ½-in. (1.25-cm) balls. Place on lightly greased cookie sheets. Bake at 350°F (175°C) for 12 to 15 minutes. Cool on racks.

Yield: 42 balls
Exchange, 1 ball: ¼ bread, ¼ fat
Calories, 1 ball: 30
Carbohydrates, 1 ball: 4 g

Whole-Wheat Pineapple Cookies

½ c.	margarine	125 mL
⅔ c.	granulated sugar replacement	180 mL
¼ c.	granulated fructose	60 mL
1	egg	1
¼ c.	crushed pineapple in juice	60 mL
1 t.	pineapple flavoring	5 mL
2 c.	whole-wheat flour	500 mL
1 t.	baking soda	5 mL

Using an electric mixer, beat margarine, sugar replacement, fructose, egg, crushed pineapple, and pineapple flavoring until well blended. In another bowl, mix flour and baking soda. Gradually beat about two-thirds of the whole-wheat mixture into the creamed mixture. Stir in remaining flour until thoroughly mixed. Shape into small patties, and place on ungreased cookie sheets. Bake at 350°F (175°C) for 10 to 12 minutes. Move to cooling racks.

Yield: 54 cookies
Exchange, 1 cookie: ¼ bread
Calories, 1 cookie: 29
Carbohydrates, 1 cookie: 4 g

Jellybean Tea Balls

½ c.	margarine	125 mL
3 T.	granulated sugar replacement	45 mL
1 T.	granulated fructose	15 mL
1 t.	vanilla extract	5 mL
1 c.	all-purpose flour	250 mL
2 T.	finely chopped dietetic jellybeans	30 mL

Using an electric mixer, beat margarine, sugar replacement, and fructose until light and fluffy. Beat in vanilla. Stir in flour until well blended. Fold in chopped jellybeans. Shape dough into ½-in. (1.25-cm) balls. Place on lightly greased cookie sheets. Bake at 350°F (175°C) for 12 to 15 minutes. Cool on racks.

Yield: 42 balls
Exchange, 1 ball: ¼ bread, ¼ fat
Calories, 1 ball: 29
Carbohydrates, 1 ball: 3 g

Great Orange Wheat Cookies

⅓ c.	frozen orange-juice concentrate	90 mL
½ c.	natural wheat & barley cereal (Grape-Nuts®)	125 mL
1 T.	margarine	15 mL
1 t.	vanilla extract	5 mL
1	egg	1
2 T.	granulated sugar replacement	30 mL
1 c.	all-purpose flour	250 mL
1 t.	baking powder	5 mL

Combine frozen orange-juice concentrate and cereal in a medium-size microwavable bowl. Cover with paper towels. Microwave on HIGH for 2 to 3 minutes. Stir in margarine, re-cover, and allow to cool for 5 minutes. Add vanilla, egg, and sugar replacement. Beat with a fork to blend completely. Stir in flour and baking powder thoroughly. Spray cookie sheets lightly with a vegetable-oil spray. Roll dough into small balls, and then into finger-shaped cookies. Place onto the greased cookie sheet. Bake at 375°F (190°C) for 15 to 17 minutes. Remove from cookie sheet, and cool on racks.

Yield: 30 cookies
Exchange, 1 cookie: ⅓ bread
Calories, 1 cookie: 24
Carbohydrates, 1 cookie: 5 g

Sweet Cornflake Balls

½ c.	margarine	125 mL
½ c.	vegetable shortening	125 mL
⅔ c.	granulated sugar replacement	180 mL
⅓ c.	granulated fructose	90 mL
1	egg	1
½ t.	vanilla extract	2 mL
½ t.	ground lemon peel	2 mL
2 c.	all-purpose flour	500 mL
¾ t.	baking soda	4 mL
½ t.	cream of tartar	2 mL
½ c.	finely crushed cornflakes	125 mL

Beat margarine and shortening together until light and fluffy. Beat in sugar replacement and fructose. Blend well. Add egg, vanilla, and lemon peel. Gradually stir flour, baking soda, and cream of tartar into creamed mixture. Cover and chill at least 3 hours. Shape dough into balls, and roll in cornflakes. Place on greased cookie sheets. Flatten each cookie by pressing it with the bottom of a glass. Bake at 350°F (175°C) for 8 to 10 minutes, or until lightly browned.

Yield: 60 cookies
Exchange, 1 cookie: ⅓ bread, ¼ fat
Calories, 1 cookie: 29
Carbohydrates, 1 cookie: 3 g

Black-Walnut Balls

¼ c.	margarine, melted	60 mL
2 T.	plain low-fat yogurt	30 mL
¾ c.	granulated sugar replacement	190 mL
¼ c.	granulated fructose	60 mL
2	eggs	2
1 t.	vanilla extract	5 mL
1½ c.	all-purpose flour	375 mL
1 t.	baking soda	5 mL
dash	salt	dash
⅓ c.	black walnuts, finely ground	90 mL

Combine melted margarine and the yogurt in a mixing bowl. Beat to blend. Beat in sugar replacement and fructose. Add eggs, one at a time, beating well after each addition. Beat in vanilla. Stir in flour, baking soda, and salt. Fold in ground black walnuts. Cover and chill for at least 2 hours. Flour your hands, and shape dough into balls. Place on lightly greased cookie sheets. Bake at 350°F (175°C) for 8 to 9 minutes. Move to cooling racks.

Yield: 42 balls
Exchange, 1 ball: ¼ bread
Calories, 1 ball: 19
Carbohydrates, 1 ball: 3 g

Cocoa Tea Balls

½ c.	margarine	125 mL
3 T.	granulated sugar replacement	45 mL
1 T.	granulated fructose	15 mL
1 t.	vanilla extract	5 mL
1 c.	all-purpose flour	250 mL
2 T.	baking cocoa	30 mL

Using an electric mixer, beat margarine, sugar replacement, and fructose until light and fluffy. Beat in vanilla. Stir in flour and cocoa until well blended. Shape dough into ½-in. (1.25 cm) balls. Place on lightly greased cookie sheets. Bake at 350°F (175°C) for 12 to 15 minutes. Cool on racks.

Yield: 42 balls
Exchange, 1 ball: ¼ bread, ¼ fat
Calories, 1 ball: 25
Carbohydrates, 1 ball: 3 g

Chocolate-Pudding Cookies

8-oz. box	buttermilk biscuit mix	227-g box
1 pkg.	sugar-free instant chocolate	1 pkg.
(4 servings)	pudding mix	(4 servings)
1 large	egg	1 large
1	egg white	1
¼ c.	vegetable oil	60 mL

Preheat oven to 350°F (175°C). Lightly grease one large or two small cookie sheets with vegetable oil. Mix biscuit mix and pudding mix together in a large mixing bowl. Beat to blend the egg with the egg white. Add egg and the ¼ c. (60 mL) of the vegetable oil to mixes. Blend well until a dough forms. Roll dough into 1-in. (2.5-cm) balls. Place balls 2 in. (5 cm) apart on the cookie sheet(s). Press the bottom of a glass onto the dough balls to flatten them slightly. Bake for about 7 to 10 minutes, or until cookies are firm. Transfer to cooling rack.

Yield: 26 cookies
Exchange, 1 cookie: ¼ bread, ⅓ fat
Calories, 1 cookie: 38
Carbohydrates, 1 cookie: 4 g

Easy Ginger-Pudding Cookies

8-oz. box	buttermilk biscuit mix	227-g box
1 pkg.	sugar-free instant vanilla-pudding	1 pkg.
(4 servings)	mix	(4 servings)
2 t.	ground ginger	10 mL
2 large	eggs	2 large
¼ c.	vegetable oil	60 mL

Preheat oven to 350°F (175°C). Lightly grease one large or two small cookie sheets with vegetable oil. Mix biscuit mix, pudding mix, and ginger together in a large mixing bowl. Slightly beat eggs together. Add eggs and vegetable oil to mixes. Blend well until a dough forms. Roll dough into 1-in. (2.5-cm) balls. Place balls 2 in. (5 cm) apart on the cookie sheet(s). Press the bottom of a glass onto the dough balls to slightly flatten balls. Bake for about 7 to 10 minutes, or until cookies are firm. Transfer to cooling racks.

Yield: 28 cookies
Exchange, 1 cookie: ¼ bread, ⅓ fat
Calories, 1 cookie: 39
Carbohydrates, 1 cookie: 4 g

Lemon-Pudding Cookies

1 c.	buttermilk biscuit mix	250 mL
1 pkg.	sugar-free instant lemon-pudding	1 pkg.
(4 servings)	mix	(4 servings)
1 large	egg, slightly beaten	1 large
¼ c.	vegetable oil	60 mL

Preheat oven to 350°F (175°C). Lightly grease one large or two small cookie sheets with vegetable oil. Mix biscuit mix and pudding mix together in a large mixing bowl. Add egg and vegetable oil to mixes. Blend well until a dough forms. Roll dough into 1-in. (2.5-cm) balls. Place balls 2 in. (5 cm) apart on the cookie sheet(s). Press the bottom of a glass onto the dough balls to flatten them slightly. Bake for about 7 to 10 minutes or until cookies are firm. Transfer to cooling rack.

Yield: 26 cookies
Exchange, 1 cookie: ¼ bread, ⅓ fat
Calories, 1 cookie: 37
Carbohydrates, 1 cookie: 4 g

Peanut-Butter Cookies

1½ c.	all-purpose flour	375 mL
¼ t.	baking soda	1 mL
dash	salt	dash
½ c.	vegetable shortening	125 mL
½ c.	peanut butter	125 mL
¾ c.	granulated brown-sugar replacement	190 mL
¼ c.	granulated fructose	60 mL
1	egg	1
1 t.	vanilla extract	5 mL

Sift together flour, baking soda, and salt; set aside. Using an electric mixer, beat together shortening and peanut butter until fluffy. Beat in brown-sugar replacement and fructose. Add egg and vanilla. Beat well. Gradually stir flour mixture into creamed mixture. Blend well. Place a piece of wax paper on a paper plate. Shape dough into balls. Place balls in a circle around the edge of the plate. Dip a fork into flour, and flatten each cookie with the tines in a crisscross design. Microwave on HIGH for 1 minute, 15 seconds. Rotate plate one-quarter turn during baking. Slip wax paper onto a cutting board, and cool cookies completely.

Yield: 42 cookies
Exchange, 1 cookie: ⅓ bread, ¼ fat
Calories, 1 cookie: 31
Carbohydrates, 1 cookie: 4 g

Deep-Chocolate Cookies

½ c.	vegetable shortening	125 mL
3 oz.	unsweetened baking chocolate	85 g
1½ c.	granulated sugar replacement	375 mL
½ c.	granulated fructose	125 mL
4	eggs	4
2 t.	vanilla extract	10 mL
2 c.	all-purpose flour	500 mL
2 t.	baking soda	10 mL
¼ t.	salt	1 mL
42	pecan halves	42

Melt shortening and baking chocolate, either in the top of a double boiler, or in a microwavable cup. Pour into a mixing bowl. Beat in sugar replacement and fructose. (Mixture will look curdled.) Add eggs, one at a time, beating well after each addition. Beat in vanilla. Stir in flour, baking soda, and salt. Cover and chill at least 2 hours. Shape dough into balls. Place balls on lightly greased cookie sheets. Break each pecan half in half again. Place small pecan piece on top of dough. Then press pecan into dough, flattening dough slightly. Bake at 350°F (175°C) for 8 to 9 minutes. Move to cooling racks.

Yield: 84 cookies
Exchange, 1 cookie: ¼ bread, ¼ fat
Calories, 1 cookie: 33
Carbohydrates, 1 cookie: 3 g

Deep-Chocolate Coconut Balls

½ c.	vegetable shortening	125 mL
3 oz.	unsweetened baking chocolate	85 g
1½ c.	granulated sugar replacement	375 mL
½ c.	granulated fructose	125 mL
4	eggs	4
2 t.	vanilla extract	10 mL
2 c.	all-purpose flour	500 mL
2 t.	baking soda	10 mL
¼ t.	salt	1 mL
⅓ c.	unsweetened flaked coconut	90 mL

Melt shortening and baking chocolate, either in the top of a double boiler or in a microwavable cup. Pour into a mixing bowl. Beat in sugar replacement and fructose. (Mixture will look curdled.) Add eggs, one at a time, beating well after each addition. Beat in vanilla. Stir in flour, baking soda, and salt. Fold in coconut. Cover and chill at least 2 hours. Shape dough into balls. Place balls on lightly greased cookie sheets. Bake at 350°F (175°C) for 8 to 9 minutes. Move to cooling racks.

Yield: 84 balls
Exchange, 1 ball: ¼ bread, ¼ fat
Calories, 1 ball: 33
Carbohydrates, 1 ball: 3 g

Chocolate Tuiles

2	egg whites, room temperature	2
⅓ c.	granulated sugar replacement	90 mL
2 T.	granulated fructose	30 mL
¼ c.	margarine	60 mL
1 oz.	semisweet baking chocolate	28 g
1 c.	all-purpose flour	250 mL
1 t.	chocolate flavoring	5 mL

Combine egg whites, sugar replacement, and fructose in a medium-size mixing bowl. Beat until foamy and well blended. Combine margarine and chocolate in a small cup; melt in microwave. Stir flour, melted margarine-chocolate mixture, and chocolate flavoring into egg mixture. Blend well. Drop onto a well-greased cookie sheet. Use a fork dipped in water to flatten dough wafer-thin. Bake at 350°F (175°C) for 8 minutes, or just until dough has lightly browned around edges. Use an oven mitt, and bend each wafer around a rolling pin. Press gently against the rolling pin for a few seconds. Slide wafer off pin, and place on cooling rack. Cool tuiles completely.

Yield: 30 tuiles
Exchange, 1 tuile: ¼ bread
Calories, 1 tuile: 21
Carbohydrates, 1 tuile: 3 g

Vanilla Tuiles

2	egg whites, room temperature	2
⅓ c.	granulated sugar replacement	90 mL
2 T.	granulated fructose	30 mL
1 c.	all-purpose flour	250 mL
¼ c.	melted margarine	60 mL
1 t.	vanilla extract	5 mL

Combine egg whites, sugar replacement, and fructose in a medium-size mixing bowl. Beat until foamy and well blended. Stir in flour, melted margarine, and vanilla. Drop onto a well-greased cookie sheet. Use a fork dipped in water to flatten dough wafer-thin. Bake at 350°F (175°C) for 8 minutes, or just until lightly browned around edges. Use an oven mitt, and bend each wafer around a rolling pin. Press gently against the rolling pin for a few seconds. Slide wafer off pin, and place on cooling rack. Cool tuiles completely.

Yield: 30 tuiles
Exchange, 1 tuile: ¼ bread
Calories, 1 tuile: 19
Carbohydrates, 1 tuile: 3 g

Almond Tuiles

2	egg whites, room temperature	2
⅓ c.	granulated sugar replacement	90 mL
2 T.	granulated fructose	30 mL
¾ c.	all-purpose flour	190 mL
¼ c.	blanched almonds, finely ground	60 mL
¼ c.	melted margarine	60 mL
1 t.	almond extract	5 mL

Combine egg whites, sugar replacement, and fructose in a medium-size mixing bowl. Beat until foamy and well blended. Stir in flour, ground almonds, melted margarine, and almond extract. Mix well. Drop onto a well-greased cookie sheet. Use a fork dipped in water to flatten dough wafer-thin. Bake at 350°F (175°C) for 8 minutes, or just until the dough has lightly browned around edges. Use an oven mitt, and bend each wafer around a rolling pin. Press gently against the rolling pin for a few seconds. Slide wafer off pin, and place on cooling rack. Cool tuiles completely.

Yield: 30 tuiles
Exchange, 1 tuile: ¼ bread
Calories, 1 tuile: 20
Carbohydrates, 1 tuile: 3 g

Currant Clusters

¼ c.	margarine, melted	60 mL
2 T.	plain low-fat yogurt	30 mL
¾ c.	granulated sugar replacement	190 mL
¼ c.	granulated fructose	60 mL
2	eggs	2
1 t.	vanilla extract	5 mL
1½ c.	all-purpose flour	375 mL
1 t.	baking soda	5 mL
dash	salt	dash
⅓ c.	currants	90 mL

Combine melted margarine and the yogurt in a mixing bowl. Beat to blend. Beat in sugar replacement and fructose. Add eggs, one at a time, beating well after each addition. Beat in vanilla. Stir in flour, baking soda, and salt. Fold in currants. Cover and chill at least 2 hours. Flour your hands, and shape dough into balls; then flatten balls slightly in the palm of your hand. Place on lightly greased cookie sheets. Bake at 350°F (175°C) for 8 to 9 minutes. Move to cooling racks.

Yield: 42 cookies
Exchange, 1 cookie: ¼ bread
Calories, 1 cookie: 20
Carbohydrates, 1 cookie: 4 g

Cinnamon Chocolate Cookies

¼ c.	margarine	60 mL
1 oz.	unsweetened baking chocolate	28 g
¾ c.	granulated sugar replacement	190 mL
¼ c.	granulated fructose	60 mL
2	eggs	2
½ t.	vanilla extract	2 mL
1 c.	all-purpose flour	250 mL
1 t.	baking soda	5 mL
1 t.	ground cinnamon	5 mL
dash	salt	dash

Melt margarine and baking chocolate, either in the top of a double boiler or in a microwavable cup. Pour into a mixing bowl. Beat in sugar replacement and fructose. (Mixture will look curdled.) Add eggs, one at a time, beating well after each addition. Beat in vanilla. Stir in flour, baking soda, cinnamon, and salt. Cover and chill at least 2 hours. Shape dough into balls. Place balls on lightly greased cookie sheets. Flatten dough slightly with fork tines. Bake at 350°F (175°C) for 8 to 9 minutes. Move to cooling racks.

Yield: 42 cookies
Exchange, 1 cookie: ⅓ bread
Calories, 1 cookie: 26
Carbohydrates, 1 cookie: 4 g

Fruited Chocolate Balls

½ c.	vegetable shortening	125 mL
3 oz.	unsweetened baking chocolate	85 g
1½ c.	granulated sugar replacement	375 mL
½ c.	granulated fructose	125 mL
4	eggs	4
2 t.	vanilla extract	10 mL
2 c.	all-purpose flour	500 mL
2 t.	baking soda	10 mL
¼ t.	salt	1 mL
⅓ c.	unsweetened dried mixed fruit	90 mL

Melt shortening and baking chocolate, either in the top of a double boiler or in a microwavable cup. Pour into a mixing bowl. Beat in sugar replacement and fructose. (Mixture will look curdled.) Add eggs, one at a time, beating well after each addition. Beat in vanilla. Stir in flour, baking soda, and salt. Fold in dried fruit. Cover and chill at least 2 hours. Shape dough into balls. Place balls on lightly greased cookie sheets. Bake at 350°F (175°C) for 8 to 9 minutes. Move to cooling racks.

Yield: 84 balls
Exchange, 1 ball: ⅓ bread
Calories, 1 ball: 27
Carbohydrates, 1 ball: 4 g

Lunch-Box Chocolate Cookies

2 c.	all-purpose flour	500 mL
2 t.	baking powder	10 mL
¼ t.	salt	1 mL
½ c.	margarine	125 mL
4 oz.	unsweetened baking chocolate	112 g
1½ c.	granulated sugar replacement	375 mL
½ c.	granulated fructose	125 mL
2 t.	brandy flavoring	10 mL
1 t.	vanilla extract	5 mL
4	eggs	4

Sift together flour, baking powder, and salt; set aside. In the top of a double boiler, melt margarine and baking chocolate. Remove top from double boiler. Add sugar replacement, fructose, brandy flavoring, and vanilla. Blend well. Add eggs, one at a time, beating well after each addition. Gradually stir in flour mixture. Mix well. Shape dough into balls, and place on greased cookie sheets. Bake at 350°F (175°C) for 15 minutes, or until set. Move to cooling racks.

Yield: 72 cookies
Exchange, 1 cookie: ⅓ bread, ½ fat
Calories, 1 cookie: 40
Carbohydrates, 1 cookie: 4 g

Vanilla-Cream Cookies

¼ c.	margarine, melted	60 mL
2 T.	plain low-fat yogurt	30 mL
¾ c.	granulated sugar replacement	190 mL
¼ c.	granulated fructose	60 mL
2	eggs	2
1 t.	vanilla extract	5 mL
1½ c.	all-purpose flour	375 mL
1 t.	baking soda	5 mL
dash	salt	dash

Combine melted margarine and the yogurt in a mixing bowl. Beat to blend. Beat in sugar replacement and fructose. Add eggs, one at a time, beating well after each addition. Beat in vanilla. Stir in flour, baking soda, and salt. Cover and chill at least 2 hours. Flour your hands, and shape dough into balls; then flatten balls slightly in the palm of your hand. Place on lightly greased cookie sheets. Using a table fork, press tines gently around the edge of each cookie. Bake at 350°F (175°C) for 8 to 9 minutes. Move to cooling racks.

Yield: 42 cookies
Exchange, 1 cookie: ⅓ bread
Calories, 1 cookie: 19
Carbohydrates, 1 cookie: 3 g

Chocolate Rounds

2 oz.	semisweet baking chocolate, melted and cooled	57 g
½ c.	margarine	125 mL
⅓ c. + 2 T.	granulated sugar replacement	120 mL
¼ c.	granulated fructose	60 mL
3	egg yolks	3
1 t.	vanilla extract	5 mL
1½ c.	all-purpose flour	375 mL
½ t.	baking powder	2 mL
dash	salt	dash

Beat chocolate and margarine until light and fluffy. Add sugar replacement and fructose; beat at least 2 minutes. Beat in egg yolks and vanilla. Gradually stir in flour, baking powder, and salt. Shape dough into small balls; then flatten balls into 1-in (2.5-cm) rounds. Place on a very lightly greased cookie sheet. Bake at 375°F (190°C) for 10 minutes, or until lightly browned. Move to cooling rack.

Yield: 36 cookies
Exchange, 1 cookie: ⅓ bread
Calories, 1 cookie: 28
Carbohydrates, 1 cookie: 4 g

Cocoa Cookies

1¾ c.	all-purpose flour	440 mL
½ c.	baking cocoa	125 mL
dash	salt	dash
¾ c.	margarine	190 mL
¼ c.	granulated brown-sugar replacement	60 mL
¼ c.	granulated fructose	60 mL
1 t.	chocolate flavoring	5 mL

Sift together flour, cocoa, and salt; set aside. Using an electric mixer, beat the margarine until fluffy. Add brown-sugar replacement and fructose. Beat well. Stir in chocolate flavoring. Gradually stir flour mixture into creamed mixture. Blend well. Place a piece of wax paper on a paper plate. Shape dough into balls; then arrange nine balls in a circle around the edge of the plate. Microwave on HIGH for 2 minutes, or until cookies are set. Rotate plate one-quarter turn once during baking. Slip wax paper onto a cutting board. Allow cookies to cool completely.

Yield: 42 cookies
Exchange, 1 cookie: ⅓ bread
Calories, 1 cookie: 29
Carbohydrates, 1 cookie: 4 g

Finger Cookies

½ c.	margarine	125 mL
⅓ c. + 2 T.	granulated sugar replacement	120 mL
¼ c.	granulated fructose	60 mL
3	egg yolks	3
1 t.	vanilla extract	5 mL
1½ c.	all-purpose flour	375 mL
½ t.	baking powder	2 mL
dash	salt	dash

Beat margarine until light and fluffy. Add sugar replacement and fructose; beat at least 2 minutes. Beat in egg yolks and vanilla. Gradually stir in flour, baking powder, and salt. Shape into balls; then roll balls between your hands into fingers. Place cookies on a very lightly greased cookie sheet. Bake at 375°F (190°C) for 10 minutes, or until lightly browned. Move to cooling rack.

Yield: 32 cookies
Exchange, 1 cookie: ⅓ bread
Calories, 1 cookie: 28
Carbohydrates, 1 cookie: 4 g

Hazelnut Puffs

½ c.	margarine	125 mL
⅓ c.	granulated sugar replacement	90 mL
⅓ c.	granulated fructose	90 mL
3	egg yolks	3
1 t.	vanilla extract	5 mL
1½ c.	all-purpose flour	375 mL
½ t.	baking powder	2 mL
dash	salt	dash
⅓ c.	finely chopped hazelnuts	90 mL

Beat margarine until light and fluffy. Add sugar replacement and fructose; beat at least 2 minutes. Beat in egg yolks and vanilla. Gradually stir in flour, baking powder, and salt. Then stir in hazelnuts. Shape dough into balls. Place on a very lightly greased cookie sheet. Bake at 375°F (190°C) for 10 minutes, or until lightly browned. Move to cooling rack.

Yield: 36 cookies
Exchange, 1 cookie: ⅓ bread, ¼ fat
Calories, 1 cookie: 29
Carbohydrates, 1 cookie: 4 g

Refrigerator Cookies

Old-Fashioned Ice-Box Cookies

½ c.	margarine	125 mL
⅓ c.	granulated sugar replacement	90 mL
¼ c.	granulated fructose	60 mL
2 T.	skim milk	30 mL
1	egg	1
1 t.	vanilla extract	5 mL
1¾ c.	all-purpose flour	440 mL
dash	salt	dash
¼ c.	finely chopped pecans	60 mL

Using an electric mixer, thoroughly cream together margarine, sugar replacement, and fructose. Beat in skim milk, egg, and vanilla. Gradually add flour and salt. Stir to completely blend. Divide dough in half. Shape each half into a 6-in. (15-cm) roll. Roll dough in the chopped pecans. Wrap each roll in wax paper. Chill dough in refrigerator overnight. Cut each roll into 18 slices. Place slices on a greased cookie sheet. Bake at 350°F (175°C) for 10 to 12 minutes. Remove from cookie sheet, and cool on rack.

Yield: 36 cookies
Exchange, 1 cookie: ⅓ bread, ½ fat
Calories, 1 cookie: 42
Carbohydrates, 1 cookie: 4 g

Thin-Lemon Refrigerator Cookies

2 c.	all-purpose flour	500 mL
½ t.	baking powder	2 mL

1 c.	margarine	250 mL
½ c.	granulated sugar replacement	125 mL
1	egg	1
1 T.	lemon juice	15 mL
½ t.	freshly grated lemon peel	2 mL

Sift together flour and baking powder; set aside. Using an electric mixer on MEDIUM, beat the margarine and sugar replacement until well blended. Add egg, lemon juice, and lemon peel. Beat well. Gradually stir dry ingredients into creamed mixture, mixing well. Divide dough in half. Shape each half into a 6-in. (15-cm) roll. Wrap each roll in plastic wrap. Chill in refrigerator overnight. Cut each roll into 30 thin slices. Place slices on ungreased cookie sheets. Bake at 375°F (190°C) for about 8 to 10 minutes, or until golden brown. Remove from cookie sheets, and place on racks.

Yield: 60 cookies
Exchange, 1 cookie: ⅓ bread, ⅓ fat
Calories, 1 cookie: 32
Carbohydrates, 1 cookie: 4 g

Creamy Cookies

1 c.	margarine	250 mL
¼ c.	granulated sugar replacement	60 mL
¼ c.	granulated fructose	60 mL
½ t.	lemon extract	2 mL
½ t.	almond extract	2 mL
½ t.	vanilla extract	2 mL
2½ c.	all-purpose flour	750 mL

Using an electric mixer on MEDIUM, beat the margarine, sugar replacement, and fructose until well blended. Beat in lemon, almond, and vanilla extracts. Gradually stir flour in creamed mixture, mixing well. Shape dough into a 13-in. (33-cm) roll. Wrap dough in plastic wrap, and refrigerate overnight. Cut roll into 48 slices. Place slices on greased cookie sheets. Bake at 350°F (175°C) for about 8 minutes, or until golden brown. Remove from cookie sheets, and place on racks.

Yield: 48 cookies
Exchange, 1 cookie: ⅓ bread, ⅓ fat
Calories, 1 cookie: 43
Carbohydrates, 1 cookie: 5 g

Cinnamon Almond Refrigerator Cookies

2¼ c.	all-purpose flour	560 mL
2 t.	ground cinnamon	10 mL
¼ t.	salt	1 mL
1 c.	margarine	250 mL
⅔ c.	granulated sugar replacement	180 mL
⅓ c.	granulated fructose	90 mL
1	egg	1
½ c.	chopped toasted almonds	125 mL

Sift together flour, cinnamon, and salt; set aside. Using an electric mixer on MEDIUM, beat the margarine, sugar replacement, and fructose until well blended. Add egg and beat well. Gradually stir dry ingredients into creamed mixture, mixing well. Stir in almonds. Divide dough in half. Shape dough into two 6-in. (15-cm) rolls. Wrap each roll in plastic wrap. Chill dough in refrigerator overnight. Cut each roll into 24 slices. Place slices on greased cookie sheets. Bake at 350°F (175°C) for about 8 to 10 minutes, or until golden brown. Remove from cookie sheets, and place on racks.

Yield: 48 cookies
Exchange, 1 cookie: ⅓ bread, ⅓ fat
Calories, 1 cookie: 33
Carbohydrates, 1 cookie: 4 g

Sunflower Cookies

1½ c.	quick-cooking oatmeal	375 mL
¾ c.	whole-wheat flour	190 mL
¼ c.	wheat germ	60 mL
½ t.	baking soda	2 mL
dash	salt	dash
½ c.	margarine	125 mL
⅔ c.	granulated sugar replacement	180 mL
⅓ c.	granulated fructose	90 mL
1	egg	1
1 t.	brandy flavoring	5 mL
½ t.	vanilla extract	2 mL
½ c.	dry-roasted sunflower seeds	125 mL
	aspartame sweetener	

Combine oatmeal, whole-wheat flour, wheat germ, baking soda, and salt in a bowl; set aside. Using an electric mixer on MEDIUM, beat the margarine, sugar replacement, and fructose until well blended. Add egg and beat well. Beat in brandy flavoring and vanilla. Stir dry ingredients into creamed mixture, mixing well. Stir in sunflower seeds. Divide dough in half. Shape each half into an 8-in. (20-cm) roll. Wrap each roll in plastic wrap. Chill in refrigerator overnight. Cut each roll into 24 slices. Place slices on ungreased cookie sheets. Bake at 375°F (190°C) for about 10 to 12 minutes, or until golden brown. Remove from cookie sheets, and place on racks. While warm, sprinkle with aspartame sweetener.

Yield: 48 cookies
Exchange, 1 cookie: 1/3 bread, 1/4 fat
Calories, 1 cookie: 29
Carbohydrates, 1 cookie: 3 g

Walnut Butterscotch Cookies

2 c.	all-purpose flour	500 mL
1/2 t.	baking soda	2 mL
1/2 t.	cream of tartar	2 mL
3/4 c.	margarine	190 mL
3/4 c.	granulated brown-sugar replacement	190 mL
1/4 c.	granulated fructose	60 mL
1	egg	1
1 t.	vanilla extract	5 mL
1/2 c.	chopped walnuts	125 mL

Sift together flour, baking soda, and cream of tartar; set aside. Using an electric mixer on MEDIUM, beat the margarine, brown-sugar replacement, and fructose until well blended. Add egg and beat well. Beat in vanilla. Gradually stir dry ingredients into creamed mixture, mixing well. Stir in walnuts. Shape dough into one 13-in. (33-cm) roll. Wrap dough in wax paper, and refrigerate at least 4 hours, or overnight. Cut roll into 54 slices. Place slices on greased cookie sheets. Bake at 400°F (200°C) for about 10 to 12 minutes, or until golden brown. Remove from cookie sheets, and place on racks.

Yield: 54 cookies
Exchange, 1 cookie: 1/3 bread, 1/3 fat
Calories, 1 cookie: 30
Carbohydrates, 1 cookie: 4 g

Cocoa Cookies

1½ c.	all-purpose flour	375 mL
½ c.	baking cocoa	125 mL
½ t.	baking soda	2 mL
⅔ c.	margarine	180 mL
¾ c.	granulated sugar replacement	190 mL
¼ c.	granulated fructose	60 mL
1	egg	1
1 t.	vanilla extract	5 mL
2 T.	skim milk	30 mL

Sift together flour, cocoa, and baking soda; set aside. Using an electric mixer on MEDIUM, beat the margarine, sugar replacement, and fructose until well blended. Add egg and beat well. Beat in vanilla. Add dry ingredients alternately with milk to creamed mixture, mixing well. Divide dough in half. Shape each half into a 7-in. (17-cm) roll. Wrap dough in wax paper, and refrigerate overnight. Cut each roll into 36 slices. Place slices on greased cookie sheets. Bake at 375°F (190°C) for about 8 minutes, or until golden brown. Remove from cookie sheets, and place on racks.

Yield: 72 cookies
Exchange, 1 cookie: ⅓ bread
Calories, 1 cookie: 26
Carbohydrates, 1 cookie: 4 g

Ice-Box Brown-Sugar Cookies

1¼ c.	all-purpose flour	310 mL
½ t.	baking soda	2 mL
¼ t.	cream of tartar	1 mL
¼ t.	salt	1 mL
½ c.	margarine	125 mL
1 c.	granulated brown-sugar replacement	250 mL
1	egg	1
1 t.	vanilla extract	5 mL
½ t.	burnt-sugar flavoring	2 mL
⅓ c.	chopped pecans	90 mL

Sift together flour, baking soda, cream of tartar, and salt; set aside. Using an electric mixer on MEDIUM, beat the margarine and brown-sugar replacement until well blended. Add egg and beat well. Beat in vanilla and burnt-sugar flavoring. Gradually stir dry ingredients into creamed mixture, mixing well. Stir in pecans. On wax paper, shape dough into a 12-in. (30-cm) roll. Roll up dough and refrigerate overnight. Cut roll into ¼-in. (8-mm) slices. Place slices on greased cookie sheets. Bake at 375°F (190°C) for about 5 to 6 minutes, or until golden brown. Remove from cookie sheets, and place on racks.

Yield: 48 cookies
Exchange, 1 cookie: ⅓ bread, ⅓ fat
Calories, 1 cookie: 33
Carbohydrates, 1 cookie: 3 g

Almond Squares

2 c.	all-purpose flour	500 mL
½ t.	baking powder	2 mL
1 c.	margarine	250 mL
¼ c.	granulated sugar replacement	60 mL
¼ c.	granulated fructose	60 mL
2 T.	water	30 mL
1 t.	almond extract	5 mL
½ t.	vanilla extract	2 mL
½ c.	chopped toasted almonds	125 mL

Sift together flour and baking powder; set aside. Using an electric mixer on MEDIUM, beat the margarine, sugar replacement, fructose, water, almond extract, and vanilla until well blended. Gradually stir dry ingredients into creamed mixture, mixing well. Stir in almonds. Cover bowl with plastic wrap, and allow to chill for 1 hour. Shape dough into a 12-in. (30-cm) roll. Wrap dough in wax paper, and push to flatten sides of roll into a square. Flatten the ends, too. Refrigerate at least 8 hours, or overnight. Cut roll into 48 slices. Place slices on ungreased cookie sheets. Bake at 350°F (175°C) for about 12 to 15 minutes, or until golden brown. Remove from cookie sheets, and place on racks.

Yield: 48 cookies
Exchange, 1 cookie: ⅓ bread, ⅓ fat
Calories, 1 cookie: 41
Carbohydrates, 1 cookie: 5 g

Brown-Sugar Slices

1¾ c.	all-purpose flour	440 mL
½ t.	baking soda	2 mL
¼ c.	margarine	60 mL
¼ c.	vegetable shortening	60 mL
1 c.	granulated brown-sugar replacement	250 mL
¼ c.	granulated fructose	60 mL
2	eggs	2
2 t.	burnt-sugar flavoring	10 mL

Sift together flour and baking soda; set aside. Using an electric mixer on MEDIUM, beat the margarine, shortening, brown-sugar replacement, and fructose until well blended. Add eggs, one at a time, beating well after each addition. Stir in burnt-sugar flavoring. Gradually stir flour mixture into creamed mixture, mixing well. Shape dough into a 12-in. (30-cm) roll. Wrap in plastic wrap, and refrigerate overnight. Cut roll into 48 slices. Place slices on greased cookie sheets. Bake at 400°F (200°C) for about 5 minutes, or until golden brown. Remove from cookie sheets, and place on racks.

Yield: 48 cookies
Exchange, 1 cookie: ⅓ bread
Calories, 1 cookie: 27
Carbohydrates, 1 cookie: 5 g

Papaya-Sugar Slices

1¾ c.	all-purpose flour	440 mL
½ t.	baking soda	2 mL
½ c.	margarine	125 mL
⅔ c.	granulated sugar replacement	180 mL
¼ c.	granulated fructose	60 mL
2	eggs	2
2 t.	vanilla extract	10 mL
2 T.	all-purpose flour	30 mL
2.5 oz.	unsweetened dried papaya, cubed	71 g

Sift together the 1¾ c. (440 mL) of flour and the baking soda; set aside. Using an electric mixer on MEDIUM, beat the margarine, sugar replacement, and fructose until well blended. Add eggs, one at a time, beating well after each addition. Stir in vanilla. Gradually stir flour mixture into creamed mixture, mixing well. Combine the 2 T. (30 mL) of flour and cubed papaya in a blender. Process on LOW or MEDIUM until papaya is powdered. Stir into cookie dough. Shape dough into a 12-in. (30-cm) roll. Wrap in plastic wrap, and refrigerate overnight. Cut roll into 48 slices. Place slices on greased cookie sheets. Bake at 400°F (200°C) for about 5 minutes, or until golden brown. Remove from cookie sheets, and place on racks.

Yield: 48 cookies
Exchange, 1 cookie: ⅓ bread
Calories, 1 cookie: 28
Carbohydrates, 1 cookie: 5 g

Pumpkin Pinwheels

1½ c.	all-purpose flour	375 mL
1 c.	quick-cooking oatmeal	250 mL
¼ t.	baking soda	1 mL
1 c.	granulated sugar replacement	250 mL
¼ c. + 2 T.	granulated fructose	60 mL + 30 mL
½ c.	margarine	125 mL
2	egg whites	2
1 c.	canned pumpkin	250 mL
1 t.	pumpkin-pie spices	5 mL

Combine flour, oatmeal, and baking soda in a small bowl; stir to mix. Set aside. Using an electric mixer, beat ¾ c. (190 mL) of the granulated sugar replacement and ¼ c. (60 mL) of the fructose with the margarine until fluffy. Beat in egg whites. Stir in flour mixture. Turn dough out onto a large piece of wax paper. Press dough into a 16 × 12 in. (40 × 30 cm) rectangle. In another bowl, combine pumpkin, pumpkin-pie spices, the remaining ¼ c. (60 mL) of sugar replacement, and the remaining 2 T. (30 mL) of fructose. Blend thoroughly. Spread pumpkin mixture over flattened dough. Roll dough, beginning at the narrow end. Wrap in wax paper; freeze overnight or until firm. Cut frozen dough into 48 slices. Place slices on greased cookie sheets. Bake at 400°F (200°C) for 8 to 9 minutes, or until golden brown. Move to cookie racks, and cool completely.

Yield: 48 cookies
Exchange, 1 cookie: ⅓ bread
Calories, 1 cookie: 38
Carbohydrates, 1 cookie: 6 g

Black-Walnut Chocolate Cookies

2½ c.	all-purpose flour	625 mL
2 t.	baking powder	10 mL
½ t.	salt	2 mL
½ c.	margarine	125 mL
¾ c.	granulated sugar replacement	190 mL
½ c.	granulated fructose	125 mL
1	egg	1
1 t.	vanilla extract	5 mL
½ t.	black-walnut flavoring	2 mL
2 oz.	unsweetened baking chocolate, melted and cooled	57 g
¼ c.	skim milk	60 mL
½ c.	chopped black walnuts	125 mL

Sift together flour, baking powder, and salt; set aside. Using an electric mixer on MEDIUM, beat the margarine, sugar replacement, and fructose until well blended. Add egg and beat well. Beat in vanilla, black-walnut flavoring, and baking chocolate. Add dry ingredients alternately with milk to creamed mixture, mixing well. Stir in black walnuts. Divide dough in half. Shape each half into an 8-in. (20-cm) roll. Wrap in wax paper, and refrigerate at least 4 hours or overnight. Cut each roll into 30 slices. Place slices on greased cookie sheets. Bake at 350°F (175°C) for about 10 to 12 minutes. Remove from cookie sheets, and place on racks.

Yield: 60 cookies
Exchange, 1 cookie: ⅓ bread, ½ fat
Calories, 1 cookie: 50
Carbohydrates, 1 cookie: 5 g

Rolled & Pressed Cookies

Cardamom Maple Spritz Cookies

1 c.	vegetable shortening	250 mL
½ c.	granulated sugar replacement	125 mL
¼ c.	granulated fructose	60 mL
1	egg	1
1 t.	vanilla extract	5 mL
1 t.	maple flavoring	5 mL
2½ c.	all-purpose flour	625 mL
2 t.	ground cardamom	10 mL
½ t.	baking powder	2 mL
dash	salt	dash

Using an electric mixer, beat shortening until light. Combine sugar replacement and fructose in a bowl; stir to mix. Gradually beat sugar-replacement mixture into creamed shortening. Beat in egg, vanilla, and maple flavoring. Combine flour, cardamom, baking powder, and salt in a mixing bowl; stir to mix. Gradually stir flour mixture into creamed mixture. Press dough from a cookie press (use thin setting or small tip) onto ungreased cookie sheets, following press manufacturer's directions. Bake at 375°F (190°C) for 8 to 10 minutes, or until edges of cookies are delicately browned. Move to cooling racks.

Yield: 75 cookies
Exchange, 1 cookie: ¼ bread
Calories, 1 cookie: 19
Carbohydrates, 1 cookie: 3 g

Oatmeal Thins

1 c.	all-purpose flour	250 mL
½ t.	baking soda	2 mL
¼ t.	salt	1 mL
½ c.	vegetable shortening	125 mL
⅓ c.	granulated brown-sugar replacement	90 mL
2 T.	granulated fructose	30 mL
¼ c.	low-fat milk	60 mL
1 c.	quick-cooking oatmeal	250 mL

Sift together flour, baking soda, and salt; set aside. Beat shortening, brown-sugar replacement, and fructose until mixture is light and fluffy. Add milk and beat well. Gradually add flour mixture to creamed mixture. Stir to blend completely. Stir in oatmeal. Divide dough in half. Roll out dough on a floured surface to a scant ¼-in. (8-mm) thickness. Cut into 18 forms, using a floured 2-in. (5-cm) cutter. Place forms on greased cookie sheet. Roll out remaining dough and repeat cutting. Bake at 350°F (175°C) for 10 minutes, or until lightly browned. Move to cooling rack.

Yield: 36 cookies
Exchange, 1 cookie: ⅓ bread
Calories, 1 cookie: 24
Carbohydrates, 1 cookie: 4 g

Apple Oatmeal Cookies

1 c.	all-purpose flour	250 mL
1 t.	apple-pie spices	5 mL
½ t.	baking soda	2 mL
¼ t.	salt	1 mL
½ c.	margarine	125 mL
⅓ c.	granulated sugar replacement	90 mL
2 T.	granulated fructose	30 mL
¼ c.	water	60 mL
1 c.	quick-cooking oatmeal	250 mL
⅓ c.	unsweetened dried apple slices, ground fine	90 mL

Sift together flour, apple-pie spices, baking soda, and salt; set aside. Beat margarine, sugar replacement, and fructose until mixture is light and fluffy. Add water and beat well. Gradually add flour mixture to creamed mixture. Stir to blend completely. Stir in oatmeal. Divide dough in half. Roll out dough on a floured surface to a scant ¼-in. (8-mm) thickness. Cut into 18 forms, using a floured 2-in. (5-cm) cutter. Place on a greased cookie sheet. Roll out remaining dough and repeat cutting. Bake at 350°F (175°C) for 10 minutes, or until lightly browned. Move to cooling rack.

Yield: 36 cookies
Exchange, 1 cookie: ⅓ bread
Calories, 1 cookie: 28
Carbohydrates, 1 cookie: 5 g

Basic-Form Cookie

2 c.	all-purpose flour	500 mL
3 t.	baking powder	15 mL
½ t.	salt	2 mL
½ c.	margarine	125 mL
¾ c.	granulated sugar replacement	190 mL
¼ c.	granulated fructose	60 mL
2	eggs	2
1 t.	vanilla extract	5 mL

Sift together flour, baking powder, and salt; set aside. Cream margarine. Add sugar replacement and fructose; beat well. Add eggs, one at a time, beating well after each addition. Beat in vanilla. Gradually stir flour mixture into creamed mixture. (You may have to knead the last amount of flour into dough.) Cover and chill dough for at least 1 hour. Divide dough in half. Roll out each half of the dough on floured surface to scant ¼-in. (8-mm) thickness. Cut dough with a floured 1½-in. (3.7-cm) cookie cutter. Place cookies on a greased cookie sheet. Bake at 400°F (200°C) for 8 minutes or until golden brown. Move to cooling rack.

Yield: 30 cookies
Exchange, 1 cookie: ½ bread
Calories, 1 cookie: 41
Carbohydrates, 1 cookie: 8 g

Peanut Cookies

2 c.	all-purpose flour	500 mL
3 t.	baking powder	15 mL
½ c.	margarine	125 mL
¾ c.	granulated sugar replacement	190 mL
¼ c.	granulated fructose	60 mL
2	eggs	2
1 t.	vanilla extract	5 mL
⅓ c.	salted peanuts, finely ground	90 mL

Sift together flour and baking powder; set aside. Cream margarine. Add sugar replacement and fructose; beat well. Add eggs, one at a time, beating well after each addition. Beat in vanilla. Gradually stir flour mixture into creamed mixture; mix well. Stir in ground salted peanuts. Cover and chill dough at least 1 hour. Divide dough in half. Roll out each half of the dough on floured surface to scant ¼-in. (8-mm) thickness. Cut dough with a floured 1½-in. (3.7-cm) cookie cutter. Place cookies on a greased cookie sheet. Bake at 400°F (200°C) for 8 minutes, or until golden brown. Move to cooling rack.

Yield: 30 cookies
Exchange, 1 cookie: ½ bread
Calories, 1 cookie: 41
Carbohydrates, 1 cookie: 8 g

Basic Spritz Cookies

1 c.	vegetable shortening	250 mL
½ c.	granulated sugar replacement	125 mL
¼ c.	granulated fructose	60 mL
1	egg	1
1 t.	vanilla or almond extract	5 mL
2¼ c.	all-purpose flour	560 mL
½ t.	baking powder	2 mL
dash	salt	dash

Using an electric mixer, beat shortening until light. Combine sugar replacement and fructose in a bowl; stir to mix. Gradually beat sugar-replacement mixture into creamed shortening. Beat in egg and vanilla. Combine flour, baking powder, and salt in a mixing bowl; stir to mix. Gradually stir flour mixture into creamed mixture. Press dough from a cookie press (use thin setting or small tip) onto ungreased cookie sheets, following press manufacturer's directions. Bake cookies at 375°F (190°C) for 8 to 10 minutes, or until edges of cookies are delicately browned. Move to cooling racks.

Yield: 70 cookies
Exchange, 1 cookie: ⅓ bread
Calories, 1 cookie: 23
Carbohydrates, 1 cookie: 2 g

Spice Spritz Cookies

2¼ c.	all-purpose flour	560 mL
¼ t.	baking soda	1 mL
1 t.	ground cinnamon	5 mL
½ t.	ground ginger	2 mL
½ t.	ground allspice	2 mL
½ t.	ground nutmeg	2 mL
¼ t.	ground cloves	1 mL
¼ t.	salt	1 mL
½ c.	margarine	125 mL
⅓ c.	granulated sugar replacement	90 mL
3 T.	granulated fructose	45 mL
1	egg	1
¼ c.	liquid fructose	60 mL

Sift together flour, baking soda, cinnamon, ginger, allspice, nutmeg, cloves, and salt; set aside. Using an electric mixer, beat margarine until light. Add granulated sugar replacement and granulated fructose. Beat until fluffy. Beat in egg and liquid fructose. Gradually beat flour mixture into creamed mixture. Press dough from a cookie press onto ungreased cookie sheets, following press manufacturer's directions. Bake at 350°F (175°C) for 8 to 10 minutes, or until cookies are lightly browned. Move to cooling racks.

Yield: 75 cookies
Exchange, 1 cookie: ⅓ bread
Calories, 1 cookie: 21
Carbohydrates, 1 cookie: 2 g

Butter-Flavored Spritz Cookies

2½ c.	all-purpose flour	625 mL
½ t.	baking powder	2 mL
¼ t.	salt	1 mL
1 c.	margarine	250 mL
½ c.	granulated sugar replacement	125 mL
¼ c.	granulated fructose	60 mL
1	egg	1
1½ t.	butter flavoring	7 mL

Sift together flour, baking powder, and salt; set aside. Using an electric mixer, beat margarine until light. Combine sugar replacement and fructose in a bowl; stir to mix. Gradually beat sugar-replacement mixture into creamed margarine. Beat in egg and butter flavoring. Gradually stir flour mixture into creamed mixture. Press dough from a cookie press (use thin setting or small tip) onto ungreased cookie sheets, following press manufacturer's directions. Bake cookies at 375°F (190°C) for 8 to 10 minutes, or until edges of cookies are delicately browned. Move to cooling racks.

Yield: 80 cookies
Exchange, 1 cookie: ⅓ bread
Calories, 1 cookie: 22
Carbohydrates, 1 cookie: 3 g

Wheat-Germ Cookies

2¼ c.	all-purpose flour	560 mL
3 t.	baking powder	15 mL
½ t.	salt	2 mL
¼ c.	wheat germ	60 mL
½ c.	margarine	125 mL
¾ c.	granulated sugar replacement	190 mL
¼ c.	granulated fructose	60 mL
2	eggs	2
1 t.	vanilla extract	5 mL

Sift together flour, baking powder, and salt. Stir in wheat germ; set aside. Beat margarine, sugar replacement, and fructose until light and fluffy.

Add eggs, one at a time, beating well after each addition. Beat in vanilla. Gradually stir flour mixture into creamed mixture. Mix well. Cover and chill dough for at least 1 hour. Divide dough in half. Roll out each half of the dough on floured surface to scant ¼-in. (8-mm) thickness. Cut dough with a floured 1½-in. (3.7-cm) cookie cutter. Place cookies on a greased cookie sheet. Bake at 400°F (200°C) for 8 minutes, or until golden brown. Move to cooling rack.

Yield: 30 cookies
Exchange, 1 cookie: ½ bread
Calories, 1 cookie: 42
Carbohydrates, 1 cookie: 9 g

Holiday Star Cookies

2 c.	all-purpose flour	500 mL
⅛ t.	ground nutmeg	0.5 mL
⅛ t.	ground cinnamon	0.5 mL
½ c.	margarine	125 mL
¾ c.	granulated sugar replacement	190 mL
¼ c.	granulated fructose	60 mL
2	eggs	2

Sift together flour, nutmeg, and cinnamon; set aside. Using an electric mixer, beat together margarine, sugar replacement, and fructose until light and fluffy. Add eggs, one at a time, beating well after each addition. Gradually stir flour into creamed mixture. Cover and chill overnight. Divide dough in half; then roll out each half on lightly floured surface to ⅛-in. (4-mm) thickness. Cut with a small star cookie cutter. Place on greased cookie sheets. Bake at 350°F (175°C) for 10 to 12 minutes. Move to cooling racks.

Yield: 96 cookies
Exchange, 1 cookie: ¼ bread
Calories, 1 cookie: 17
Carbohydrates, 1 cookie: 2 g

Brown-Sugar Press Cookies

1 c.	margarine	250 mL
¾ c.	granulated brown-sugar replacement	190 mL
1	egg yolk	1
1 t.	vanilla extract	5 mL
½ t.	caramel flavoring	2 mL
¼ t.	salt	1 mL
2 c.	all-purpose flour	500 mL

Using an electric mixer, beat margarine in a large mixing bowl. Gradually add brown-sugar replacement, beating until light and fluffy. Beat in egg yolk, vanilla, caramel flavoring, and salt. Stir in flour, Chill for at least 2 hours. Press dough from cookie press onto ungreased cookie sheets, following press manufacturer's directions. Bake at 350°F (175°C) for 8 to 10 minutes. Move to cooling racks.

Yield: 60 cookies
Exchange, 1 cookie: ⅓ bread
Calories, 1 cookie: 23
Carbohydrates, 1 cookie: 3 g

Caraway Diamonds

1½ c.	all-purpose flour	375 mL
2 T.	vegetable shortening	30 mL
2 T.	margarine	30 mL
¼ c.	granulated sugar replacement	60 mL
1	egg	1
½ t.	vanilla extract	2 mL
½ t.	crushed caraway seeds	2 mL

Sift flour, and set aside. Using an electric mixer, beat together shortening, margarine, and sugar replacement until light and fluffy. Beat in egg and vanilla. Gradually add flour to creamed mixture. Stir in caraway seeds. Roll out dough on lightly floured surface to ⅛-in. (4-mm) thickness. Cut into 2-in. (5-cm) diamonds. Place dough on greased cookie sheets. Bake at 325°F (165°C) for 10 to 12 minutes. Move to cooling racks.

Yield: 40 cookies
Exchange, 1 cookie: ¼ bread
Calories, 1 cookie: 21
Carbohydrates, 1 cookie: 3 g

EXCHANGE LISTS

The reason for dividing food into six different groups is that foods vary in their carbohydrate, protein, fat, and calorie content. Each exchange list contains foods that are alike – each choice contains about the same amount of carbohydrate, protein, fat, and calories.

The following chart shows the amount of these nutrients in one serving from each exchange list.

Exchange List	Carbohydrate (grams)	Protein (grams)	Fat (grams)	Calories
Starch/Bread	15	3	trace	80
Meat				
Lean	–	7	3	55
Medium-Fat	–	7	5	75
High-Fat	–	7	8	100
Vegetable	5	2	–	25
Fruit	15	–	–	60
Milk				
Skim	12	8	trace	90
Lowfat	12	8	5	120
Whole	12	8	8	150
Fat	–	–	5	45

As you read the exchange lists, you will notice that one choice often is a larger amount of food than another choice from the same list. Because foods are so different, each food is measured or weighed so the amount of carbohydrate, protein, fat, and calories is the same in each choice.

You will notice symbols on some foods in the exchange groups. Foods that are high in fiber (3 grams or more per exchange) have this 🐚 symbol. High-fiber foods are good for you. It is important to eat more of these foods.

Foods that are high in sodium (400 milligrams or more of sodium per exchange) have this 🐚• symbol; foods that have 400 mg or more of sodium if two or more exchanges are eaten have this ★ symbol. It's a good idea to limit your intake of high-salt foods, especially if you have high blood pressure.

If you have a favorite food that is not included in any of these groups, ask your dietitian about it. That food can probably be worked into your meal plan, at least now and then.

The Exchange Lists are the basis of a meal-planning system designed by a committee of the American Diabetes Association and The American Dietetic Association. While designed primarily for people with diabetes and others who must follow special diets, the Exchange Lists are based on principles of good nutrition that apply to everyone. Copyright © 1989 American Diabetes Association Inc., and The American Dietetic Association. The American Diabetes Association has many publications to help you live better with diabetes. For more information, or to order a free publications catalog, call the American Diabetes Association.

1
STARCH/BREAD LIST

E ach item in this list contains approximately 15 grams of carbohydrate, 3 grams of protein, a trace of fat, and 80 calories. Whole grain products average about 2 grams of fiber per exchange. Some foods are higher in fiber. Those foods that contain 3 or more grams of fiber per exchange are identified with the fiber symbol 🌿.

You can choose your starch exchanges from any of the items on this list. If you want to eat a starch food that is not on this list, the general rule is that:

- 1/2 cup of cereal, grain or pasta is one exchange
- 1 ounce of a bread product is one exchange

Your dietitian can help you be more exact.

CEREALS/GRAINS/PASTA

🌿 Bran cereals, concentrated (such as Bran Buds® All Bran®)	1/3 cup
🌿 Bran cereals, flaked	1/2 cup
Bulgur (cooked)	1/2 cup
Cooked cereals	1/2 cup
Cornmeal (dry)	2 1/2 Tbsp.
Grape-Nuts®	3 Tbsp.
Grits (cooked)	1/2 cup
Other ready-to-eat unsweetened cereals	3/4 cup
Pasta (cooked)	1/2 cup
Puffed cereal	1 1/2 cup
Rice, white or brown (cooked)	1/3 cup
Shredded wheat	1/2 cup
🌿 Wheat germ	3 Tbsp.

DRIED BEANS/PEAS/LENTILS

🌿 Beans and peas (cooked) (such as kidney, white, split, blackeye)	1/3 cup
🌿 Lentils (cooked)	1/3 cup
🌿 Baked beans	1/4 cup

STARCHY VEGETABLES

🌿 Corn	1/2 cup
🌿 Corn on cob, 6 in. long	1
🌿 Lima beans	1/2 cup

🌿 Peas, green (canned or frozen)	1/2 cup
🌿 Plantain	1/2 cup
Potato, baked	1 small (3 oz.)
Potato, mashed	1/2 cup
🌿 Squash, winter (acorn, butternut)	1 cup
Yam, sweet potato, plain	1/3 cup

BREAD

Bagel	1/2 (1 oz.)
Bread sticks, crisp, 4 in. long × 1/2 in.	2 (2/3 oz.)
Croutons, lowfat	1 cup
English muffin	1/2
Frankfurter or hamburger bun	1/2 (1 oz.)
Pita, 6 in. across	1/2
Plain roll, small	1 (1 oz.)
Raisin, unfrosted	1 slice (1 oz.)
Rye, pumpernickel	1 slice (1 oz.)
Tortilla, 6 in. across	1
White (including French, Italian)	1 slice (1 oz.)
Whole wheat	1 slice (1 oz.)

🌿 3 grams or more of fiber per exchange

CRACKERS/SNACKS

Animal crackers	8
Graham crackers, 2 1/2 in. square	3
Matzoh	3/4 oz.
Melba toast	5 slices
Oyster crackers	24
Popcorn (popped, no fat added)	3 cups
Pretzels	3/4 oz.
✔ Rye crisp, 2 in. × 3 1/2 in.	4
Saltine-type crackers	6
✔ Whole-wheat crackers, no fat added (crisp breads, such as Finn®, Kavli®, Wasa®)	2-4 slices (3/4 oz.)
Taco shell, 6 in. across	2
Waffle, 4 1/2 in. square	1
✔ Whole-wheat crackers, fat added (such as Triscuit®)	4-6 (1 oz.)

STARCH FOODS PREPARED WITH FAT

(Count as 1 starch/bread exchange, plus 1 fat exchange.)

Biscuit, 2 1/2 in. across	1
Chow mein noodles	1/2 cup
Corn bread, 2 in. cube	1 (2 oz.)
Cracker, round butter type	6
French fried potatoes, 2 in. to 3 1/2 in. long	10 (1 1/2 oz.)
Muffin, plain, small	1
Pancake, 4 in. across	2
Stuffing, bread (prepared)	1/4 cup

2
MEAT LIST

ach serving of meat and substitutes on this list contains about 7 grams of protein. The amount of fat and number of calories varies, depending on what kind of meat or substitute you choose. The list is divided into three parts based on the amount of fat and calories: lean meat, medium-fat meat, and high-fat meat. One ounce (one meat exchange) of each of these includes:

	Carbohydrate (grams)	Protein (grams)	Fat (grams)	Calories
Lean	0	7	3	55
Medium-Fat	0	7	5	75
High-Fat	0	7	8	100

You are encouraged to use more lean and medium-fat meat, poultry, and fish in your meal plan. This will help decrease your fat intake, which may help decrease your risk for heart disease. The items from the high-fat group are high in saturated fat, cholesterol, and calories. You should limit your choices from the high-fat group to three (3) times per week. Meat and substitutes do not contribute any fiber to your meal plan.

🐷 *Meats and meat substitutes that have 400 milligrams or more of sodium per exchange are indicated with this symbol.*

Meats and meat substitutes that have 400 mg or more of sodium if two or more exchanges are eaten are indicated with this symbol.

LEAN MEAT AND SUBSTITUTES
(One exchange is equal to any one of the following items.)

Beef:	USDA Select or Choice grades of lean beef, such as round, sirloin, and flank steak; tenderloin; and chipped beef 🍖	1 oz.
Pork:	Lean pork, such as fresh ham; canned, cured or boiled ham 🍖 Canadian bacon 🍖 , tenderloin.	1 oz.
Veal:	All cuts are lean except for veal cutlets (ground or cubed). Examples of lean veal are chops and roasts.	1 oz.
Poultry:	Chicken, turkey, Cornish hen (without skin)	1 oz.
Fish:	All fresh and frozen fish	1 oz.
	Crab, lobster, scallops, shrimp, clams (fresh or canned in water)	2 oz.
	Oysters	6 medium
	Tuna ★ (canned in water)	1/4 cup
	Herring ★ (uncreamed or smoked)	1 oz.
	Sardines (canned)	2 medium
Wild Game:	Venison, rabbit, squirrel	1 oz.
	Pheasant, duck, goose (without skin)	1 oz.
Cheese:	Any cottage cheese ★	1/4 cup
	Grated parmesan	2 Tbsp.
	Diet cheeses 🍖 (with less than 55 calories per ounce)	1 oz.
Other:	95% fat-free luncheon meat 🍖	1 1/2 oz.
	Egg whites	3 whites
	Egg substitutes with less than 55 calories per 1/2 cup	1/2 cup

🍖 *400 mg or more of sodium per exchange*

★ *400 mg or more of sodium if two or more exchanges are eaten*

MEDIUM-FAT MEAT AND SUBSTITUTES
(One exchange is equal to any one of the following items.)

Beef:	Most beef products fall into this category. Examples are: all ground beef, roast (rib, chuck, rump), steak (cubed, Porterhouse, T-bone), and meatloaf.	1 oz.
Pork:	Most pork products fall into this category. Examples are: chops, loin roast, Boston butt, cutlets.	1 oz.
Lamb:	Most lamb products fall into this category. Examples are: chops, leg, and roast.	1 oz.
Veal:	Cutlet (ground or cubed, unbreaded)	1 oz.
Poultry:	Chicken (with skin), domestic duck or goose (well drained of fat), ground turkey	1 oz.
Fish:	Tuna ★ (canned in oil and drained)	1/4 cup
	Salmon ★ (canned)	1/4 cup
Cheese:	Skim or part-skim milk cheeses, such as:	
	Ricotta	1/4 cup
	Mozzarella	1 oz.
	Diet cheeses 🍖 (with 56-80 calories per ounce)	1 oz.
Other:	86% fat-free luncheon meat ★	1 oz.
	Egg (high in cholesterol, limit to 3 per week)	1
	Egg substitutes with 56-80 calories per 1/4 cup	1/4 cup
	Tofu (2 1/2 in. × 2 3/4 in. × 1 in.)	4 oz.
	Liver, heart, kidney, sweetbreads (high in cholesterol)	1 oz.

🍖 *400 mg or more of sodium per exchange*

400 mg or more of sodium if two or more exchanges are eaten

HIGH-FAT MEAT AND SUBSTITUTES

Remember, these items are high in saturated fat, cholesterol, and calories, and should be used only three (3) times per week.

(One exchange is equal to any one of the following items.)

Beef:	Most USDA Prime cuts of beef, such as ribs, corned beef	1 oz.
Pork:	Spareribs, ground pork, pork sausage 🐷 (patty or link)	1 oz.
Lamb:	Patties (ground lamb)	1 oz.
Fish:	Any fried fish product	1 oz.
Cheese:	All regular cheeses, such as American 🐷, Blue 🐷, Cheddar , Monterey Jack , Swiss	1 oz.
Other:	Luncheon meat 🐷 , such as bologna, salami, pimento loaf	1 oz.
	Sausage 🐷 , such as Polish, Italian smoked	1 oz.
	Knockwurst 🐷	1 oz.
	Bratwurst	1 oz.
	Frankfurter 🐷 (turkey or chicken)	1 frank (10/lb.)
	Peanut butter (contains unsaturated fat)	1 Tbsp.

Count as one high-fat meat plus one fat exchange:

Frankfurter 🐷 (beef, pork, or combination)	1 frank (10/lb.)

🐷 *400 mg or more of sodium per exchange*

400 mg or more of sodium if two or more exchanges are eaten

3
VEGETABLE LIST

ach vegetable serving on this list contains about 5 grams of carbohydrate, 2 grams of protein, and 25 calories. Vegetables contain 2-3 grams of dietary fiber. Vegetables which contain 400 mg or more of sodium per exchange are identified with a ⬛ symbol.

Vegetables are a good source of vitamins and minerals. Fresh and frozen vegetables have more vitamins and less added salt. Rinsing canned vegetables will remove much of the salt.

Unless otherwise noted, the serving size for vegetables (one vegetable exchange) is:

1/2 cup of cooked vegetables or vegetable juice
1 cup of raw vegetables

Artichoke (1/2 medium)
Asparagus
Beans (green, wax, Italian)
Bean sprouts
Beets
Broccoli
Brussels sprouts
Cabbage, cooked
Carrots
Cauliflower
Eggplant
Greens (collard, mustard, turnip)
Kohlrabi
Leeks

Mushrooms, cooked
Okra
Onions
Pea pods
Peppers (green)
Rutabaga
Sauerkraut ⬛
Spinach, cooked
Summer squash (crookneck)
Tomato (one large)
Tomato/vegetable juice ⬛
Turnips
Water chestnuts
Zucchini, cooked

Starchy vegetables such as corn, peas, and potatoes are found on the Starch/Bread List.

⬛ 400 mg or more of sodium per exchange

4
FRUIT LIST

Each item on this list contains about 15 grams of carbohydrate and 60 calories. Fresh, frozen, and dried fruits have about 2 grams of fiber per exchange. Fruits that have 3 or more grams of fiber per exchange have a 🌿 symbol. Fruit juices contain very little dietary fiber.

The carbohydrate and calorie content for a fruit exchange are based on the usual serving of the most commonly eaten fruits. Use fresh fruits or fruits frozen or canned without sugar added. Whole fruit is more filling than fruit juice and may be a better choice for those who are trying to lose weight. Unless otherwise noted, the serving size for one fruit exchange is:

1/2 cup of fresh fruit or fruit juice
1/4 cup of dried fruit

FRESH, FROZEN, AND UNSWEETENED CANNED FRUIT

Apple (raw, 2 in. across)	1 apple
Applesauce (unsweetened)	1/2 cup
Apricots (medium, raw)	4 apricots
Apricots (canned)	1/2 cup, or 4 halves
Banana (9 in. long)	1/2 banana
🌿 Blackberries (raw)	3/4 cup
🌿 Blueberries (raw)	3/4 cup
Cantaloupe (5 in. across)	1/3 melon
(cubes)	1 cup
Cherries (large, raw)	12 cherries
Cherries (canned)	1/2 cup
Figs (raw, 2 in. across)	2 figs
Fruit cocktail (canned)	1/2 cup
Grapefruit (medium)	1/2 grapefruit
Grapefruit (segments)	3/4 cup
Grapes (small)	15 grapes
Honeydew melon (medium)	1/8 melon
(cubes)	1 cup
Kiwi (large)	1 kiwi
Mandarin oranges	3/4 cup
Mango (small)	1/2 mango
🌿 Nectarine (2 1/2 in. across)	1 nectarine
Orange (2 1/2 in. across)	1 orange
Papaya	1 cup
Peach (2 3/4 in. across)	1 peach, or 3/4 cup
Peaches (canned)	1/2 cup or 2 halves
Pear	1/2 large, or 1 small

Pears (canned)	1/2 cup, or 2 halves
Persimmon (medium, native)	2 persimmons
Pineapple (raw)	3/4 cup
Pineapple (canned)	1/3 cup
Plum (raw, 2 in. across)	2 plums
🌿 Pomegranate	1/2 pomegranate
🌿 Raspberries (raw)	1 cup
🌿 Strawberries (raw, whole)	1 1/4 cup
🌿 Tangerine (2 1/2 in. across)	2 tangerines
Watermelon (cubes)	1 1/4 cup

DRIED FRUIT

🌿 Apples	4 rings
🌿 Apricots	7 halves
Dates	2 1/2 medium
🌿 Figs	1 1/2
🌿 Prunes	3 medium
Raisins	2 Tbsp.

FRUIT JUICE

Apple juice/cider	1/2 cup
Cranberry juice cocktail	1/3 cup
Grapefruit juice	1/2 cup
Grape juice	1/3 cup
Orange juice	1/2 cup
Pineapple juice	1/2 cup
Prune juice	1/3 cup

🌿 *3 or more grams of fiber per exchange*

5
MILK LIST

Each serving of milk or milk products on this list contains about 12 grams of carbohydrate and 8 grams of protein. The amount of fat in milk is measured in percent (%) of butterfat. The calories vary, depending on what kind of milk you choose. The list is divided into three parts based on the amount of fat and calories: skim/very lowfat milk, lowfat milk, and whole milk. One serving (one milk exchange) of each of these includes:

	Carbohydrate (grams)	Protein (grams)	Fat (grams)	Calories
Skim/Very Lowfat	12	8	trace	90
Lowfat	12	8	5	120
Whole	12	8	8	150

Milk is the body's main source of calcium, the mineral needed for growth and repair of bones. Yogurt is also a good source of calcium. Yogurt and many dry or powdered milk products have different amounts of fat. If you have questions about a particular item, read the label to find out the fat and calorie content.

Milk is good to drink, but it can also be added to cereal, and to other foods. Many tasty dishes such as sugar-free pudding are made with milk. Add life to plain yogurt by adding one of your fruit exchanges to it.

SKIM AND VERY LOWFAT MILK

skim milk	1 cup
1/2% milk	1 cup
1% milk	1 cup
lowfat buttermilk	1 cup
evaporated skim milk	1/2 cup
dry nonfat milk	1/3 cup
plain nonfat yogurt	8 oz.

LOWFAT MILK

2% milk	1 cup fluid
plain lowfat yogurt (with added nonfat milk solids)	8 oz.

WHOLE MILK

The whole milk group has much more fat per serving than the skim and lowfat groups. Whole milk has more than 3 1/4% butterfat. Try to limit your choices from the whole milk group as much as possible.

whole milk	1 cup
evaporated whole milk	1/2 cup
whole plain yogurt	8 oz.

6
FAT LIST

Each serving on the fat list contains about 5 grams of fat and 45 calories.

The foods on the fat list contain mostly fat, although some items may also contain a small amount of protein. All fats are high in calories and should be carefully measured. Everyone should modify fat intake by eating unsaturated fats instead of saturated fats. The sodium content of these foods varies widely. Check the label for sodium information.

UNSATURATED FATS

Avocado	1/8 medium
Margarine	1 tsp.
★ Margarine, diet	1 Tbsp.
Mayonnaise	1 tsp.
★ Mayonnaise, reduced-calorie	1 Tbsp.

Nuts and Seeds:

Almonds, dry roasted	6 whole
Cashews, dry roasted	1 Tbsp.
Pecans	2 whole
Peanuts	20 small or 10 large
Walnuts	2 whole
Other nuts	1 Tbsp.
Seeds, pine nuts, sun-flower (without shells)	1 Tbsp.
Pumpkin seeds	2 tsp.

Oil (corn, cottonseed, safflower, soybean, sunflower, olive, peanut)	1 tsp.
Olives	10 small or 5 large
Salad dressing, mayonnaise-type	2 tsp.
Salad dressing, mayonnaise-type, reduced-calorie	1 Tbsp.
Salad dressing (oil varieties)	1 Tbsp.

🖝 Salad dressing, reduced-calorie	2 Tbsp.

(Two tablespoons of low-calorie salad dressing is a free food.)

SATURATED FATS

Butter	1 tsp.
★ Bacon	1 slice
Chitterlings	1/2 ounce
Coconut, shredded	2 Tbsp.
Coffee whitener, liquid	2 Tbsp.
Coffee whitener, powder	4 tsp.
Cream (light, coffee, table)	2 Tbsp.
Cream, sour	2 Tbsp.
Cream (heavy, whipping)	1 Tbsp.
Cream cheese	1 Tbsp.
★ Salt pork	1/4 ounce

🖝 *400 mg or more of sodium per exchange*

★ *400 mg or more of sodium if two or more exchanges are eaten*

Index